EXPLAINING TECHNOLOGY HOW INFLUENCES JOBS NUMBER REDUCES

JOHN LOK

Made with ♥ on the Notion Press Platform
www.notionpress.com

Contents

Preface

Introduction

Nowadays, human technology had been experiencing improvement rapid stage, such as mobile has been improved to reach smart phone stage. Smart phone invention may let human applies internet channel to send email, read e-books, listen music, watch movie to enjoy leisure activities. Whether may smart phone and internet invention influence global jobs number reduce. Also for rocket invention example, rockets can bring space tourism leisure, but it also replace human choose to travel in ourselves earth. So, it may influence global travel industry jobs reduce.

However, if human ourselves technology can continue to develop, whether it can help global economy to continue grow in long term. But, when global economic growth, whether technology can brings global any jobs reduce. In my this book, I shall attempt to indicate some new technological invention whether it can influence global jobs number reduces.

Prologue

Table of content

Robots invention whether they can help organizations to raise efficiencies or inefficiencies?

Why social behavior may influence organizational strategy needs to be changed ?

Reasons why human behavior may influence economic recession or growth ?

How employee behavior influences organizational development?

Artificial intelligent Human clever and art creating ability methods

Why does technology raise online products sale demand and reduces shops products sale demand?

Does car technological development reach mature stage to help economic development?

Chapter 5 Space tourism how influence travel industry employees number reduce

● Psychology and economic environment changing both factors influence whole space tourism market leisure desire

● space tourism strategy p.111-120

(1) safe space tourism journey

(2) reduction cost expense plan

(3) achieve any space tourism mission plan

Methods to raise space traveler number

● What is the prediction space travelling passenger desire method ?

● The prediction of price factor influences space traveler number

The influential factors persuade travelers choose space tourism p.121-135

● Raising space tourism leisure consumption strategies

Research how to raise space traveler individual leisure desire

Space travel marketing strategy p.136-150

(1) On concept of spacecraft design aspect

● Outsourcing spacecraft concept design strategy

(2) On deciding misson aspect

(4) On target audience prediction aspect

(3) On space tourism leisure organization managment aspect

(5) On space objective aspect

● Space tourism leisure behavioral economic consumption model

(1) Economic environment variable factor
(2) Space tourism leisure journey management factor

● Space tourism market moral ethic risk threats

(1) Potential accidents aspect
(2) Space tourism destinations and space tourism entertainment facilities safe arrangement challenges aspect
(3) Space tourism market competition challenge aspect

● Can space tourism business bring economy benefits

(1) On space resource benefit aspect
(2) On education benefit aspect

● What are the tangible social and economic benefits brought from space tourism?

● Space flight safe factor
● Space exploration organization mission and strategy
● Space exploration organization communication strategy
● Space exploration organization's human space life science factor

● What is human space life science strategy?
● How can human space life science strategy implement?
● Situation analysis

What are space life science strategy goals?

Health innovation goal

Prediction on future trends in human space flight and future space human life science strategy relationship.

Why does Japan space organization consider space human life science?

CHAPTER ONE

Technology how influences traditional jobs number reduces

Nowadays, our global economy seems to continue grow, but it also has possible to bring recession by any factors. This question concerns whether either human behavior can influence future global social economic growth or recession or technology can influence future global social economic growth or recession more? I shall attempt to indicate evidences to explain as below:

Firstly, on the one hand, when one country can manufacture new technological products, e.g. laptops, war weapons (non-manual driving flying war air planes, space rocket, smart phone etc. different kinds of high technological products. For America example, US is one export high technogical products country. When its these different kinds of high development products manufacturers can sell to local and overseas customers. Then, they may earn high profit from both. Alsn US government can charge high profit tax from these high technologicalproducts manufacturers, when they can attract global many customers to buy their any kinds of high technological products. So, it seems that high technological products manufacturers may help US government and US high technological products manufacturers to earn more US technological products sale income. Moreover, technology can help US country to grow up its economic development in long term, due to US manufacturers can concentrate on effort to invent any kinds of new technological products in order to persuade global buyers to chooce to buy their products in preference.

However, but on the other hand, I feel human behavior, such as talent high technological products inventors , they are the beginning main factor to help US to grow economy. The reason is because US which any kinds of high technological products must need talent human product scientists) themselves idea to invention. If themselves idea can influence global high technological products buyers feel needs to buy to use. Then, they must choose to buy US country's any kinds of these products in preference. So, talent high technological product scientists will be US future economic growth source. If one high technological product scientists did wrong idea to the high technological
product manufacturers to manufacture the kind technological products. They can not influence global buyers feel needs to buy the kind of high technological product to use. Then, whose
idea of innovationm may not help US to develop itself eocnomy.

Hence, such as technological product case example, talent product scientists their idea innovation factor can bring more influential to US future economic growth easily. So, I conclude this criticism to explain why human behavior is more important factor to compare technology to influence the country's economy, because if the high technological product inventor whose dreams and iea to invent the kind of high technological product, if it can influence users feel useful feeling, e.g. smart phone product, it can attract phone users buy to use because it can use internet to gather global data, or read online news, read electonic books, listen music, watch movie, take photos, know the day weather, send and receive email, download document etx. different kinds of fuctions. SO, can let phone users feel smart phones can replace past traditional innovation of mobile phones and smart phones can influence global mobile users feel human ourselves can make phone calls in convenient in anywhere. Hence, smart phone product manufacturers can help themselves countries to earn high GDP income and increase high profit tax to give themselves governments. Otherwise, the traditional mobile phone products can not persuade phone buyers to choose to buy forever, because
they lack more functions to compare smart phones.

So, it explains why smart phone users personal using phone behavior is more important to influence the country's economy because when global every family begin to feel to use smart phones is themselve daily habit, they need smart phone to help them to do any matters, instead of general phone call at streets. So, their using smart phone behavior will influence they feel often need to change new mobdel of smart phone invention of product to replace old model of smart phone. Consequently, smart phone manufacturers need to continue to invent new and more functions of new model of smart phone products to satisfy future global smart phone users' need. Henvce, smart phone users' habitual using new model smart phone using behavior may bring global smart phone manufactuers long term manufacturing benefits in order to increase sale number chance. So, smart phone is one kind of high technological product may help any smart phone manufacturing countries to grow up economic growth easily. Also, smart phone inventor individual

idea and smart phone improvement skillful technology and smart phone user individual frequent chaning new model using behavior which may be main factors to

influence the country's smart phone sellers sale number. Such as, UK, US, Germany , CHina. Korea , they are global main smart phone manufacturers.

Economists call it " production -side growth" , which means that most companies, most of the time, made their (such as those countries smart phone manufacturers profit by cutting the cost of production). If these countries' smart phone manufacturers can coopcrate to research how to improve more new functions of new model of smart phones to sellin global smart phone market. Consequently, it is possible that their production of smart phone cost may be influenced to reduce. Then, themselves future invention of new model

of smart phone product sale price may also be influenced to reduce, due to reducing production cost. Then, the global smart phone buyers number may be influenced to increase by reducing smart phone production cost. When these manufacturing smart phone countries, every year , their smart phone sale number Ccan increase to double time , even more.

I believe that smart phone technological product may help these countries to earn more profit tax, if these countries smart phone manufacturers need to research how to improve future smat phone functions to satisfy global future smart phone user individuia; " frequent changing new model of smart phone habitual satisfactory need". So, future smart phone technological product may be one kind of high technological product to help the smart phone manufacturing countries themselves economic growth.

Ecommerce may also help the country to grow economy. In the past, before twentieth century , this efficiency extends to the ways our economic goods spread around the country and the world. As the begining of the twentieth century , most markets , more local, most people bought things made nearby. But with the expansion system and then commercial air travel and the super-efficiency of containerized shipping, markets became national and eventually, global. Till to first century, since internet technological invention, it brings economic chance to let any countries local merchants may apply web-store internet platform to help them to sell products to overseas buyers. They only need click to the overseas seller whose web store and then they canpay visa to buy the kind of product frm the online seller's web-store. So, many merchants , they own webstores to let overseas buyers can pay visa to buy the kind of product from themselves web-stores at their home countries conveniently. Then, the owning " more number of web-store sellers " countries government will have possible to earn high profit tax from these local webstore sellers. So, ecommercal sale internet technological platforms and global online buyers purchase behaviors , these two factors mau also influence the country's economy. If the country had many people like to buy any kinds of products from webstore, then they may influence the " owning more number of online sellers countries" their online seller profit increases, whether it is more or less sale number. Hence, whether e-commerce technology may help the country's government to grow GDP in technological product sale view. It depends on whether the country owns how many number of online sellers as well as how many online buyers number both for their products choice purchase chance. For example, when the country own high number people like to spend more time to stay at home to use internet. They do not like to walk on streets, they like to listen music and read books at homes more than going outside to do sports. Then, the country's people individual living habit will influence they choose to apply webstores to buy any things, if the country had

many people like to stay at homes more than leaving homes. SO, individual living behavior may also influence the country economy on online purchase view.

Finally, nowadays, some economists indicate that human ourselves behavior may be as full participants in Earth's cyclical processes of life and economy.

They think that human behavior, such as we are rational economic man, social adaptable humans, our daily behaviuors may bring direct or indirect influences

to global economy growth or recession. For share market example, before 21 century, share buyers need to go to banks or finance companies or share markets to buy the
company's shares. But, since 21 century, smart phone technological products had been invented. Nowadays global many share inventors began to choose to use smart phones
to buy and sell any companies shares in any time and any where conveniently. So, smart phone invention had brought indirect influence to global share buyers'carrying on
sale and buying shares investing behavioral transactions in preferable choice. SO, smart phones and internet invention may influence global many share investors
shares investment behavior and investment attitude change. It seems that this both new technological invention can encourage future share investors accept to
apply smart phones to carry on shares buying and selling transactions more than visiting finance companies to enquire share agents their idea because, they can
apply smart phone to observe global any shares whether their prices will rise up or fall down immedicately. SO, smart phone and internet will changfe future share investors investment
behavior.

Two economic sociologists, DOnald Mackenzie and Yuval Miko, decided to reseach how share traders behaviors, however, by interviewing some of the share traders themselves. What did they discover? That the theory's increasing accuracy ovdr time was because the share traders had started
to behave as if the theory ware true and so were using the model's predicted prices as a benchark for selling, their owning bids. FInancial economics, they
concluded " helped create in reality the kind of markets, it posited in theory. Ans as financial markets later learned, when those theories turn out to
be flowed. If rational economic man can reshape our behavior in financial markets, he is vary likely to be reshaped our behavios in past. Hence, smart phone can influence future share buyers to do shares buying and selling decision in short time as well as it can persuade global share markets shares purchase number increases to bring economic growth.

Learning invisible hand economy theory

How may " inivisible hand " factor influence the smart phone manufacturer products demand number increase?

The invisible hand is for the law of supply and demand explains how the pull and push of these two factors serve to benefit sciety as a whole. In simple, every consumer choose to buy the product, he/she pursues to earn the most more interest to the manufacturer needs to produce the product as its product may be of the greatest value to let the consumer intends only his/her own gain, led by an invisible hand to promote the product to let the consumer to make satisfaction to choose to buy the product.

In behavioral economic view, the invisible hand to the product manufacturer may be " the consumer whose satisfactory feeling to use the product".So, the invisible hand meant that ir can not be touch , seen, it only brings feeling to let the consumer to feel. This feeling to the product is very mportant factor to excite the consumer to choose to buy the product, e.g. smart phone product the smart phone buyer's invisible hand factor may include: The smart phone can link to app to use internet service, download documents from smart phone , taking phonoes, watching movie, listening music, clock time etc. function, seeling different countries street locations, instead of general mobile talking function.

So, all of above factors will be future new smart phone main " invisible hand" factors to excite future smart phone buyers to make purchase decision to choose to buy the kind of smart phone among different kinds of smart phone products innovation , when they are manufactured to promote to smart phone market to sell.

So, in smart phone market supply and demand view, the smart phone manufacturer needs to innovate new smart phone products in order to let smart phone buyers fee its news phone buyers feel itsnew smart phone products have unique functions or features to excite its smart phone buyers to choose to buy its new kind of smart phone products, because smart phone buyers will be influences to make final smart phone purchase decision by invisible hand factors from smart phone different new function

.

Smart phone manufacturers need to innovate many new functions o future new kinds of smart phone manufacturing in order to bring new invisible hand satisfactory feeling to let any one smart phone buyer to feel whose new smart phone can bring the most unique satisfactory feeling to let them to feel. So, smart phone 's invisible hand factor is main influential factor to bring smart phone manufacturer's new smart phone demand number will increase or decrease. If the smart phone manufacturer can often innovate its smart phone products to let smart phone buyers feel more using satisfactory feeling to its new kind of smart phone more than its other similar kinds of smart phone manufacturers. Then, the smart phone manufacturer ought raise its smart phone purchase number demand easily.

What is smart phone opportunity cost?

Hence, the concept of opportunity cost factor means smart phone manufacturers need to forgone opportunities of time cost , design new kinds of smart phone products, e.g. smart phone pictures, colour and shape , future smart phone manufacturers need to concentrate more time to research how to innovate new featurers and function to let every potential smart phone buyers to bring more functions using satisfactory feeling in order to attract they choose to buy its smart phone product.

On conclusion, opportunity cost to smart phone manufacturers may be forgone spend more time on smart phone design, colour choice, shape choice aspects. Smart phone manufacturers need to spend more time on innovate new feature and function aspects in order to satisfy future smart phone using needs in global competitive smart phone smart.

- Why can (AI) driving machine learning system main factor influence driving consumer individual desires ?

Driving consumer expectations are hard to measure or predict driving attitudes and driving behaviors in (AI) non-manual driving vehicles market. Artificial intelligence is another kind of computer science development to apply intelligent vehicle market. Why do driving consumers feel need to buy any kinds of (AI) auto driving vehicles to drive to replace manual driving vehicles on the roads? What are (AI) auto driving features different to manual driving features?

(AI) is the recreation of cognitive functions in computers; it enables machines to perform tasks like humans and perhaps even better than human. In the real world, scientists develop the technological singularity, in which a superintelligence emerges with unfold human consequences.

Professionals in many industries are intensely interested in the specifics of what (AI) can do today, and how can it helps. They are considering the impact of applied (AI), in which computers are used to address a particular problem, extracting and utilizing patterns found in large volumes of data. Of all (AI)'s subfields, machine learning is attracting the most attention. I shall explain why (AI) machine learning system is the main factor to lead consumers feel need to buy any (AI) products to use. Such as below:

For smartphone, fraud detection to medical diagnosis etc. applied (AI) technological products examples. (AI) machine learning systems can help any one of these products to do any exceed general computer learning systems which (AI) learning systems can do any skills to supply (AI) users to use to compare computer learning systems can not do any skills to supply compute users to use. It seems that (AI) machine learning system is the unique feature to attract consumer consideration in technological product market.

An term for different types of learning, and can be accomplished using different techniques. This has led to a perception that all marketing teams should have (AI) to bring a unified personalized customer experience, when consumers choose to buy any (AI) products to feel what are the different or unique characteristics to compare general computer products. Such as (AI) product has this unique machine learning characteristics, we can predict (AI) and machine learning is connected to influence consumers to feel needs.

Furthermore, over the same time period, and in contrast to predictions for roles in many industries. (AI) won't take the place of marketers and merchandisers themselves although it is already a new value to analytical and strategic marketing skills to persuade consumers to buy any (AI) products. It means different kinds of (AI) products will have different machine learning effort and unique characteristics to attract consumers to choose to buy them to use. Such as, when intelligent vehicles need have unique road driving or sea transportation or flying machine learning system when they are applied on these three kinds of transportation tool aspects. They need have good response safety driving and immediate response learning systems to avoid any boats or air planes or vehicles to crash to them to reduce accident occurrences immediately on any one of either road or sky or sea journey environment.

- What rail passengers really want rail innovation improvement

Public transport systems, such as rail provides benefits including less traffic congestion, less pollution, safe travels, lower expenditures , less effort and better predictability in comparison to road transport. In fact, bus and train riders experience the most negative emotions in comparison with other transport modes, such as private cars , walking and cycling. Hence, technology has the potential to bring about the changes, needed to increase efficiency of rail transport, e.g. cost-effective ways to improve the quality of public transport and increase ridership may involve comfort and convenience improvement, or technology has the potential to provide more up-to-date information and customized service to train passengers and therefore improve the rail journey experience . On the overall, passenger journey , e.g. the importance of automated traveller information systems, and electronic fare payment collection systems can bring rail passengers look for this information in different interfaces from localized displays installed on platforms to smartphone applications.

Moreover, technology can also improve fare collection and management which of made manually can be prone to error, and time consuming , unified cards, smartphones can make it easier for rail passengers to obtain ticket, with the potential to increase the user satisfaction with the rail system. Because rail passengers demand not only pre-trip information for planning their travels, but also information during journeys, such as punctuality, connections and platform allocation. One extensive review indicates that accurate communication, for example, giving effective way finding information, can optimize passengers' experience with public transport.

Also, technology can facilitate the process of finding free seats on trains, which is a current demand from rail passengers and the cause of stress during the boarding process. IN fact, many rail passengers have specific preferences regarding seats and would appreciate having control of where to sit. So, navigation and way finding information can be delivered directly to passengers to inform where they could stand aiming to board less busy carriages, for example, choosing to travel on a less crowded train, or spreading themselves out on the platform before boarding in respond to crowding information, e.g. smartphones are frequently used by passengers of public transport and can make waiting times seem shorter. Furthermore specific system features designed for train passengers have the potential to improve the journey experience of the travelling public.

CHAPTER TWO

Investing in office technology can reduce employees number

Why ought any kinds of businesses need to invest in technology to offices when businessmen began to do businesses? The reason is simple, such as any offices need email to communicate to let different departments staffs can contact to do any tasks in short time. So, email can replace telephone calling communication channel between departments in offices. Moreover, for paper files, electronic files may replace to keep to save any office confident documents or general memos, letters, reports etc. documents. So, paper printing number may reduce. Even some businesses began to sell their products from online webstores to let customers to pat visa to buy their products from their webstores conveniently. Hence, computer technology is essential to nowadays any kinds of businesses offices.

The best are developed with the entire project-focused organization in mind. For example, a question on resourcing could involve looking a cariety of systems and files with no way to automatically generate the rught combination of data. Hence, any business offices ought need a single, centralised database which keeps accounting, project and even HR information and can integrate data when required.

ON the office investing in technology web-based system with mobile access benefit, due to investing globalization and pressure on fee rates means staff are in the office less

frequently than ever. A web-based system means data can be accessed from PCs and networked laptops with no other software needed. So, instead of

offices can apply laptops and intra-internet communication technological tool, which can also offer the option of a mobile applications suite which means personnel working on -site can enter timesheet and expense reports from laptops, even when not connected to the central data base. This helps minimise time delays, streamlining the billing process and improving cash flow. So, office mobile onlinesite technology may help thme to bring real-time , easy access benefits. For exmaple, if a staff is still making decisions based on information that is seven or eight weeks old, the staff will be surprised by the power of having real-time information at the
staff's fingertips. At any time this will give the staff an accurate "snapshot" of the health of the staff's
project, enabling the staff to take preventive action if the problems arise before it is too late.

This visualisation ensures that all key stakeholders can identify project problems immediately they happen . It's also an ideal way for directors or other managers to grab headline information before a short notice meeting, for example, all of office laptop, mobile intra-internet, onsite technology may help to ensure more targeted decisions and better project control. Hence, office technology may help any business offices to save more time deal urgent tasks daiuly. It means that office technology may help any offices to save much time in long term.

For some businesses office technology may help their businesses to manage on projects to achieve rapid finishing in short time, such as all projects of harbour construction business aspect, some projects may face complex to prolong time to finish. SO, defining a discipline as " complex project management assumes that one can find projects cause of complexity". Also, any the harbour business projects do not really exist. The term project is a contract used to describe a particular human activity. Hence, if the harbour construction company managers can let its all harbour construction managers to apply mobile onsite technology, intra-internet communication channel to do daily communication tasks in short time between their different construction teams. Then, these new harbour onsite mobile intra-internet communication technology ought help all
onsite harbour construction managers can supervise all harbour onsite workers to construct all harbour construction projects in short time efficiently and effectively.

Sp, on-site mobile intra-internet communication technology may be future construction industry which a kind of essential onsite mobile intra-

internet communication
technoogy.Moreover, on-site mobile intra-internet communication technology can bring future construction industry on time to save cost and construction quality
improvement benefits. Due to increasingly construction industry and clients demand more for less and this is in a traditionalty high risk industry. The problem of construction and its relatively slow pace of change seem to stem from its competive building living demand role in providing building buyer value. With its attendant professions, it is often too remote from the customers' experience of their buildings.

When if the construction company really knew how to add value for building clients? What if the construction firm could improve productivity among those using the building?
How much is that worth? What if the school could improve performance of students in shcools and the recovery of patients in hospitals? Such improvements represent much cost
benefits that could mean that the building pays for itself. However, nowadays building technology can bring these key benefical features to any construction companies, such as
value success are committed leadership providing the vision, suitable values and effective shared processes.

How office technology brings intelligent thinking to office staffs? Finally, I beleive that if the company can invest technology in office. It will bring intelligent thinking to office staffs in order to improve efficient and performance, because investing in office technology , which is a way to reduce risk without
going over the top through effective use of the company networks. Why can office technology working environment can help staffs to bring intelligent thinking in order to
improve performance and raise efficiency?

The reason of office technology working environment can excite staffs their intelligent thining to be raise. What's lacking is a way of mitigating against these risks and doing so cost- effectively. Because more recently, a new stage has been reached where office staffs rely not only on their technical and business knowledge, but now have methodologies and tools so sophisticated that they can forward predict and control any office projects to finish before due date more easily.Hence, with good technical knowledge, sound business underatanding, a good way of methodologies, and training in the very latest software technology to hand, these are the not investing in office technology staffs, those who still find it impossible to deliver projects successfully more easily before any their office projects finishing due date. What needs to be addressed to change this situation? The main factors critical to improve office staffs performance and improve efficiency, the non-investing in office technology working environment ought to

changed to invest technology to office working environment in order to excite staff individual working emotion to bring raising efficiency, even improve performance effectiveness.

ON conclusion, any offices need to invest technology to offices in order to bring " improving technical skill to staffs their working environment", because they need to know that skill does not equate to competence , and there fore, a competence and therefore a competency based assessment is essential so that a

prospective office employee knowledge and understanding, attitude and skills can be evaluated. So, technological office can help managers to evaluate office employee

individual job skill more easily in order to make decision whether skill is high or low to let high skillful staffs can continue to be trained to work in offices as well as fire the low skillful staffs. So, when the office can attempt to spend more money to invest to its office working environment, it means that the organization should be investing in training for permanent staffs in the scarce skills working markets. A small investment in office technology can reap significant benefits further down the live, such as planning for skills scarcity on investing nowadays office technological working environment.

CHAPTER THREE

Can non-manual driving cars influences global public transport drivers number reduce

Nowadays, non-manual driving car invention may influence traditional car market development. In car development history, human had been habitly driving gas energy cars, but since battery energy cars invention, it can influence environmental protection car buyers feel gas energy cars may pollute global air. So, many different countries car buyers begin to choose to buy battery energy cars to replace traditional gas energy cars to drive. For example, US, Uk, China , they haver many big cities, their different cities living car buyers had begun to choose to buy battery energy cars to replace their old gas energy cars to drive to different destinations from their living cities every day.

So, it seems that nettergy energy cars had been beginning to replace some old gas energy cars in some countries cities, e.g. China Shanghai large cities, US, New York, Washington large cities, UK London large city. However, it brings these questions: Can non-manual driving cars may dominate future traditonal gas energy cars market? Because, cattergy energy cars bring environmental protection advantages to reduce air pollution. So, battery energy cars may influence nowadays many gas energy car buyers to choose to buy battery energy cars to replace gas energy cars to replace gas energy cars to drive to avoid air pollution problem serious occurrence in our future societies.

In car market demand and supply view, I assume that if future many gas energy car owners accept to battery energy cars can reduce air polution continue influences our health when we often breathe dirty air due to gas energy cars' emission. Hence, I estimate the demand number of battery energy cars pollution will be influenced to increase by air pollution. If future global air pollution will continue seriously influence global human health, it will influence global many car owners make choice either not buy any cars to drive, they will choose to catch public transport tools, e.g. bus, tram ,ferry, taxi, underground train etc. to go to anywhere or they will choose to buy battery energy cars to avoid gas continue pollute air to influence our health. So, it seems that battery energy cars will replace traditional gas energy cars to cause gas energy cars demand number decreases and battery energy cars demand number increases.

The other questions concern: Can battery energy cars influence future non-manual driving cars demand number reduces? Can non-manual driving cars replace battery energy cars and gas energy cars to dominate global car market?

In fact, non-manual driving cars may let many lazy car drivers or car buyers do not need to drive their cars, robots may help them to drive cars when they are sitting in themselves cars. So , they may read books, lsten music or sleep when their non-manual driving cars are still running on the roads. Although, non-manual driving cars can let many lazy car drivers feel comfortable and free when they are sitting in themselves cars. But non-manul driving cars can let they feel not safe, when robots help they to drive cars.

It means that their lifes are dominated by robots. However, traffic accidents may occur in any time, if robots help them to drive their cars in whole road journey time. So, they will feel more dangerous to compare they drive themselves cars on road busy time. Moreover, non-manual driving cars also need gas energy. So, non-manual driving cars still cause air pollution when many non-manual driving cars are being driving on the roads.

Hence, non-manual driving cars can also let environmental protection drivers feel that they can cause air pollution when they are driven on the roads by robots. Otherwise, battery energy cars must not pollute air , because they are using battery charge energy to replace gas or oil energy. Moreover battery energy cars won't let many car drivers feel safe to drive themselves cars on the road, due to they can still drive themselves cars and they won't need robots to help them to drive cars on the roads.

On conclusion, it seems that battery energy cars can attract many car buyers to choose to buy more than the kinds of both non-manual driving cars and gas energy cars. In supply and demand view, if future non-manual driving car manufacturers hope to raise sale price and demand purchase number. Unless, they can reduce their future any kinds of non-manual driving manufacture number to less than battery energy cars sale number to let future non-manual driving buyers feel that they can not buy any kinds of non-manual driving cars easily if they make purchase decision to buy them leter. Then, any kinds of non-manual driving cars prices may be influenced to raise to sell more easier when car buyers feel their supply number will begin to reduce to sell in global non-manual driving car market. However, future battery energy cars will be non-manual driving cars main competitive choice target to global car buyers. So, non-manual driving cars will be difficult to dominate the primary car choice tool to car buyers in future global car market.

CHAPTER FOUR

Technology how influences organizational jobs number reduces

Human Behavioral network job brings social economic benefits

What does human network job mean ? Why may human network job be popular? Why human network job behavior may influence economy ? Nowadays internet is popular to use. We can apply internet to find data , search any new things, even earn money. Why does internet may become huma network job source. For example, e-publish may be one kind of new human network job. Any authors may apply internet channel to help them to sell electronic or paper books from e-publisher web store. They may apply facebook, you tub etc. any online channel to promote themselves new books to let new readers to know whether when they may buy themselves favourable new topic books to read

from electronic publisher web store.

Thus, future electronic publisher industry may help any authors to build internet network platform to help them to sell and promote ot advertise their any one new electronic or paper book topic to let global any one reader to choose to buy their any new topic books from electronic publisher web store easily and conveniently. However, it implies that electronic network platform author may be one kind of future new human network job in our societies.

How electronic network platform author job may bring economy benefit in macro economy view? A person can have few friends, contacts and still be very influential if these few

friends and contacts are themselves highly influential, e.g. one author must not need to know any one reader in global society. When they like to choose any electronic books from electronic internet network platform. They may become the author's any one topic book buyer, when they feel the author's any one topic book is fun and attract they make decision to buth the strange author whose the topic book from electronic book publisher's platform web store conventiently in short time. Although, they are strangers, they do not know themselves , but the reader can understand what it way that made Google from writing platofrm to create new creative mind and typing network job method to replace traditional hand writing book method for global authors. It will be one kind of new human network writing job.

Hence, global any one reader can apply an innovative search engine , such as google.com to find whether whom author personal new topic books are value to read from internet.

Then, the electroniuc publisher's web store may be new book store platform sale network to help the author to sell many electronic or paper books from electronic network platform

in short time. So, internet may be future new network plaform to help global any one author to create network writing job absolutely. Furthermore, internet may be popular social media

to help any one author to build goold relationship between his/her readers. It is one kind of new network, human network job. New authors do not need to buy many paper books to prepare to put in any one book shop warehouse. Their every book can print on demand to reduce out of book stock in any one book shop. They may choose to sell either electronic books or paper books both from any one book publisher web store. So, electronic network platform may be one kind of good writing channel to help human authors to create income and it can also help authors to bring new creative mind and new topic fun content books to let readers to know and buy to read from electronic publisher network platform.

Why does human behavior may be one kind of new human network job to bring global economic advantages. ALthough, it may be free income or without inocme, but the person does the network behavior, his/her behavior may be bring advantages to influence many other people's health. For this case, when a worker in a coffee shop in an airport gets a vaccination aganinst the flu, it does not only helps him or her stay healthy, but also helps the many travellers who might otherwise have been inflected if that workers caught the flu. So, the externality , the result implies the vaccination of even a part of a community conveys benefits to the whole community. For example, governments pay special attention to the vaccinations of school children, teachers, health mothers, and the elderly, categories of people particularly susceptible not only to catching, but also to transmitting a disease.

It is not accidential that governments are heavily involved with vaccination . When there are externalities, free market, fail to persuade individual incentives with society's

their the worker's decision of whether to get a vaccine ends up attracting whether other people get sick. The workers might not fully take all these other people's potential suffering into account when making her or his vaccination decision.

As Stanford University does many suggestions, understand this and tries to help them make the right decisions and so providers free flu vaccines for its staff and students.

Small pockets of unvaccinated individuals can allow a disease to gain a spread more widely well-being. For example, parent weighing the costs and benefits of a vaccine for their child is not always thinking of the consequences of that vaccination to other people. THese are markets in which subsidizing or regulating behavior can make everyone better off. Because the reason for requiring that a child be vaccinated before enrolling in school is not just to protect that child, because each child's vaccination affects others via potential contagions.

Robots take our jobs behavioral and economy influences

Robot job behavior brings economy influences

If one day robots can replace human to do simple, even complex jobs. They will bring what influences to our global societial economy.The popular economic refrain declares that the

global middle class is dying and robots will soon take our jobs, e.g. shopping center customer service jobs, library service jobs, cinema ticket sale jobs, restaurant kitchen cooker jobs,

even, bus drivers, taxi drivers etc. public transport driving jobs, accountant, doctors etc. professional jobs. Whether it is beautiful or petty matter if our future societies have many human jobs can be replaced to do from robots.

Businessman must may reduce to employ employees and reduce to pay salary or wage, when robots can be replaced to do their employees tasks. But, societies must bring unemployement rate rises , due to societies will have many people loss jobs when their employers choose to buy robots to serve their clients or do any office tasks or customer service or cleaning etc. tasks.

In micro economy view, employers may save money in long term, but in macro economy view, it will cause unemployment ratio rises , even crime rate rises when there are many people lose
jobs in societies. These models of doom, though, fail to account for the hundreds of businesses riding the waves of change in their industries when robots may be invented to replace human to do many simple , even complex tasks in our future societies.

WE may image that one small factory needs to manufacture fishes canes to sell to supermarket, the small , cheaper stuff and higher margin parts of the fishes manufacture industry. Before, this factory needs to employe many human factory workers need to help every fresh customer makeing the perfect fishing gear, designed for performance, durability, and cost in order to achieve to manufacture every fish cane in whole fished processing manufacturing stages. Every worker needs to spend about 15 to twenty minutes to finish every fish cane , till to delivery to any supermarket to sell. If this fish canes manufacturing factory can apply manufacturing robots to help them to finish any one working tasks , every robot can only spend five minutes to finish whole fresh fish cane manufacturing process. Thus, every robot can
help this factory save 10 to 15 minutes time to finsh every fish cane manufacturing process. IN fact, time is money, because when every robot can help this factory to reduce 10 to 15 minutes time to compare human worker. Then, this factory can finish about 20 fish canes in one hour if it can use robot to help it to manufacture fish canes. Otherwise, if this factory still use human workers to help it to manufacture fish canes, then it can finsh about 3 to 4 fish canes in one hour. SO, the manufacturing efficiency ensures that robots must help this fish manufacturing factory to raise fish canes number more than human workers. So, in robotic behavioral economy view, manufacturing robots must help this fish canes manufacturing factory to raise fish canes manufacturing number and deliver increasing number to supermarkets to prepare to sell every day. Robots can help this fish canes manufacturing factory bring manufacturing time saving,

rising manufacturing efficiency, improving performance and reducing wages expenditure long time advantages in micro economy view. However, manufacturing robots can also bring disadvanages to society, e.g. increasing unemployment ratio, increasing crime rate,
this factory workers will lose jobs and income, they need earn social welfare from government and increasing government finance pressure in short time, even long time in macro economic view.

Stanford University graduate program in economics, Scott lecturer explained that "in demand and supply economic theory for robots supply and demand case, robots supply number increasing may influence human workers demand number decrease. It sometimes calls " the efficient frontier".
No specific human beings were mentioned in any of economics classes. As robots supply and demand in market case, They (robots) may be purely theoretical " agents" who reached to the most reasonable sale prices in order to persuade any one businessman buyer to make manufacturing robot buying decision whether robots can help him / her to bring how much saving time , saving money, saving cost, improving performance, efficiency economic benefit before he/she plans to reduce workers number when he/ she decides to apply robots to replace human workers in his/her factory or office or any service department, e.g. cinema ticket sale service, shopping center customer service, shopping center cleaning , supermarket customer service etc. service or sale tasks. When robots can replace human to do any one of these tasks in any organizations. So, robots may be human worker agents who reached to prices the way robots would react to a software
command. There was nothing that explained why some people thrived and others did n't or why truly brilliant, hardworking people could fail when much lazier folks succeeded." Having been admitted to the Stanford University graduate program in economics, Scott lecturer hoped to get his answers there.

How robots influence our future social changing? Using the right technology can be a boon to your business in this economy. For internet example, it is easier than ever to find well-matched customers all around the world, to stay in contact with them, and to more quickly design the products they want. If you focus solely on being cutting -edge, though you risk letting the technology
take over what should be very robust relationships with your customers , employees, and colleagues. IN nowaddays society, technoligical advances

and cutomation, personal
relationships in business are more crucial than ever. I mean that robots can not replace human to serve clients to let them to feel more comfortable and passion more easily. For shoe shop case example, if the shoe shop apply one robot to serve its clients to replace human shoe salesperson to serve its shoe customers. Robots ensure that they can not persuade every shoe potential buyer to make shoe buying decision more easily when robots need to contact every shoe potential buyer. The reason is simple, because robots can not touch any one shoe buyer individual emotion very easier.

If the shoe buyer needs the robots to help him/her to choose any right shoe styles when he/she can not feel himself / herself can make the most right shoe style choice decision. The robots can not replace human shoe salesperson to make shoe style choice judgement more easily. They must need longer time to analyze whether which shoe style may be the most suitable to the shoe buyer. Otherwise, human shoe salesperson may attempt to make the most right shoe style choice decision to help any one shoe buyer to chooce the most right style shoe because he/she owns shoe style sale experience, shoe style knowledge, the most important reason is that they can feel every shoe customer individual emotion to touch whether he/she will feel comfortable or happy when they attempt to help every shoe customer to seek the most right shoe style in every shoe customer whole shoe searching processing. Othwerwise, serving robots are only one machine, they can not touch or feel every shoe customer individual emotion whether he/she feel comfortable or unhappy or happy when they need to contact them in whole shoe searching processing. Hence, I believe that some tasks robots can
not repalce human staff to do very easily. Otherwise, robots may bring disadvanatges to let any one businessman to loss his/her customers, due to robots can not touch every customer
emotion to compare human staff in service tasks more easily. Robots serving customer behaviors may cause money lose and customers number lose to the shop in micro economic view.

Intellectual human economic behaviors

What does intellectual human economic behaviors mean ? I believe that when we choose or decide to do intellectual behaviors, then our societies will be influenced to bring economic growth in consequence.I shall attempt to indicate pollution case to explain how and why eithet our intellectual or foolish behaviors may bring economic growth or recession in consequence as below:

On one hand, for air pollution social case aspect example, if we only consider to buy cars to drive for working aimr or holiday leisure aim. Then, our societies air will be polluted. Our health will be influenced to bad. Our car driving behaviors may cause global environment air pollution serously. In long tiem, global air pollution will bring our bodies health to be bad. Although, ourselves car driving behaviors may bring our driving travelling leisure enjoyment and comfortable feeling in short time, also we so not need to pay public transport fare often, but we need to compensate ourselves health economic intangible loss due to air pollution , when cars number increases, dirty air will cause ouselves health to become bad.

In the result, we will need to pay more medical expenditure when we are old age, due to ourselves bodies will become bad, due to we breathe global dirty air every day, due to ourselves cars pollute air in long time, e.g. 10 to 20 years, even 30 more without limited air pollution environment. So, driving cars behavior may be one kind of human foolish behavior and our foolish behavior may bring ourselves future long time medical expenditure absolutely.

One the other hand, water pollution social aspect, if we often keep much rubblish to pollute sea, oil exploration porcessing pollute ocean , ships gas pollute ocaen, then fishes will eat polluted food and drive dirty water, due to global ocean is polluted.

In fact, because human only to conside how to buy boats to carry on leisure enjoyment activities, or catch cruises to travel on the sea. Also, oil manufacturers only consider researching anywhere to find new oil exploration places to manufacture oil product, when their oil exploration processes pollute ocarn . Consequently, global fishes drink polluted warer or eat polluted food. They will have poison. SO, human will have high chance to eat poison polluted fishes, due to fishes are poison or are polluted.

So, human is doing foolish activities, we only hope to find oil exploration places to pollute ocean or we only spend money to buy ticket to catch ships to travel anywhere in global ocean. All of these human foolish behaviors will bring pollution to global ocean. On consequently, we will need to compensate to eat polluted or dirty or poision fishes, ourselves bodies health will be bad. In long time, we need have high chance to pay medical expenditure when we are old. So, pollution case may be one good example to explain how and why human foolish behavior may influence ourselves future need to compensate serious medical loss.

All of these human foolish behavior will bring pollution to global ocean. On consequently, we will need to compensate to eat polluted or dirty or poison fished , ourselves bodies health will be bad. In long time, we will have high chance to pay medical expenditure, when we are old. So, pollution case may be one good example to explain how and why human ourselves intellectual or foolish behaviors may influence future long time economic loss or economic growth or recession in micro and micro economic view.

On another water pollution aspect hand, if we often keep rubbish to sea, oil exploration processing pollutes ocean and ships' gas pollute ocean, then fishes will eat polluted food and drink dirty water, due to fishes will eat polluted food and drink dirty sea water because the global ocean is polluted seriously.

In fact, because human only consider how to buy boats to carry on any leisure water activities, or catches cruises to travel on the sea. Also, oil manufacturers only consider any where to find oil exploratin places to manufacture oil products from ocean, when their pol exploration processes can plooute ocean. Consequently, global fishes drink polluted water or eat direty food. They will have poison. So, human will have high chance to eat poison fishes.

Otherwise, such as pollutin case, it can infuence inflation or deflation. Consequently, the reason indicates supply and demand theory. If air pollution is serious, then we will consider health issue, global cars demand number may be influenced to reduce, when global cars number demand will reduce, global car prices and supply number will need to change to fall down in order to attract or persuade global car consumers choose to make car purchase decision.

Hence, global car manufacture number and car price will be influenced to reduce, due to global air pollution issue. Consequently, deflation will occur because when the country citizen usually does not spend much extra saving money to buy car expensive goods. Money value will be low. Otherwise, if global cair pollution is not serious, human considers to buy cars to enjoy driving leisure lives. So, global car demand is influenced to increase , also global car price will also influenced to increase.

Consequently, gobal human will choose to buy cars to drive. Due to we accept to spend extra saving to buy expensive car goods. Car sale price and supply may be influenced to rise up. Money value is influenced to reduce. Inflation may be influenced, due to global car consumers number increases, we would not have extra money to spend easily. Car expensive goods expenditure influences our spending habit to avoid to make car purchase decision more easily. So, human intellectual or foolish activities may bring inflation or deflation consequency in possible indirectly in macro economic view.

On conclusion, above pollution case explain that how and why human intellectual or foolish economic behaviors may bring inflation or deflation consequency as wll as economic growth or recession consequency as well as any goods demand and supply increasing or decreasing consequency. It implies that human behavior may have indirect relationship to influence any goods demand and supply number to either increase or decrease result as well as any goods price will be influenced to increase or decrease in micro and macro economic view.

The relationship between social change and human behavior

Why does economic changes may influence human individual behavioral change? I shall attempt to indicate shopping behavior and staying at home behavior to explain their case and effect relationsip as below:

Human behavior can be influenced by economic change or economic change can be influenced by human behavior? Why does recession may influence consumers reduce shopping desire? In social recession suitation, it is possible that many people lose jobs suddenly, due to businessmen lose many customers. They need to make decision to reduce employees number in order to continue to keep businesses. Consequently, many firms (organizations) their employees may lose jobs. When they have much time, due to lose jobs, they will feel to avoid to spend too much time and money to go to shopping often. Many losing jobs people, they will often stay at homes. So, they will reduce time to go to shopping, then non essential products won't their preferable choice purchase products. Hence, recession will change many losing jobs people their shopping or consumption desires to avoid to buy non essential products often . Usually when economic boom, many people have jobs to do because consumers number must increase when many people have jobs to do. Then, many people can accept to spend money to buy non essential products often. Many people feel spend time to go to shopping can satisfy their purchase of any kinds of new products useful psychology or desire. So, recession is one good example to explain it can influence many people do not like often to leave homes to go to shopping easily. Many people like to stay at homes, becaue they feel worry about spending too much shopping time when they leave homes. Their staying home time is one good negative shopping behavior example. So, economic change may influence human individual behavior changes , they have direct cause and efect relationship in behavioral economic view.

May human behavior influence economic change? Is it possible that human behavior may bring the country social economic change in macro economic or micro behavioral economic view ? I shall indicate publishing industry example. Do you feel that if there are many students feel learning is very important when they read many books or many of students feel interesting to read or they have reading new books in habit, then it is possible that the country will have many students like to spend time to go to any book shops to choose the books, they feel that they can help they learn new knowledge. Then the country will increase students number, they often spend time to visit any one book shop every week. Their visiting book shops behavior which may become their habits. So, the country will increase students number, they often spend time to visit book shops. Also, it implies that visiting book shops behaviors may be their behavioral habits.

So, when the country has many students often spend time to visit book shops , their visiting book shops behaviors may help any one book shop to raise books sale chance. So, the country's student individual often visiting book shop behaviors, their habitual visiting book shops behaviors must may assist help any one book shop to increase books sale number absolutely.

Consequently, any one book shop , its books sale bumber must be influenced to increase to increase because the country will have many students like or feel need visit book shops habit in order to choose any suitable books to buy to read at home in order to raise themselves learning effort. When the country has many bok shops often have many students visit their book shops, then their books sale number may be influenced to increase. It explain why student individual visiting book shop behavior may help any one book shop sale number increases also.

How human productive behavior may influence economic development

May any country which citizen behavior assist themselves country development? It is one cause and effect economic question. I mean that if the country itself citicen can not concentrate mind or energy to choose to do one kind of industry in order to let themselves country can bring the most benefit, then whether the counry itself economy can bring the most serious economic benefit. I shall attempt to indicate these countries themselves indistry choice to explain whether these countries themselves citizen productive behavior may help themselves countries to achieve the

largest economic benefits. I shall indicate as below:
New Zealand farmer individual wine productive behavior
For New Zealand country example, this country concerns itself effort is foucs on farming agricultural aspect. So, this country has many farmers concentrate on farming agricultural aspect. May New Zealanders choose to spend time to produce different kinds of wines, e.g. wine or red grape wine is for the people are eating meat, or they are eating dinner.
When these New Zealanders their behaviors choose to do farming or agriculture to grow and produce different kinds of taste of white or red grape wine drinking products job. Themselves grape agriculture behavior will influence these New Zealanders themselves, they can learn how to improve different kinds of grape wine drinking products in order to achieve every kinds of white or read grape wines taste improving aim during their white or red grape producing process.
Why can New Zealander every individual white or read grape wine producers improve their white or read grape wine taste more easily? In behavioral economic view, it can explain that why any one New Zealander white or read grape wine producer can be encouraged or excited or persuaded to concentrate nervous and energy and effort to learn how to improve their white or red grape wine products easily.
In fact, New Zealand is one agricultural food export country. It has good natural environment resource , e.g. land, seed to provide any one farmer to produce themselves any kinds of agricultrual food products, e.g. fruit, or wine food products. Because New Zealanders know themselves country has enough natural resource . So, in common, many New Zealanders choose to attempt to do farming agricultural jobs in order to export themselves any kinds of fruit or meat or wine products to overseas or sell to domestic in order to earn profit.
So, when these New Zealand farmers number has been increasing every year. This country farmers will feel themsleves competition between this New Zealand farmers themselves are serious due to they may feel New Zealanders choose to do agriculture businesses in order to export themselves different kinds of farming food to overseas or sell to local to earn profit.
Hence, when many New Zealand farmers feel that farmers number has been increasing every year. They will feel themselves competition is serious. They must need to spend much time and nervous and effort to research what method is the best how to produce the best taste of white or red grape

wine products in order to let local or overseas wine buyers to choose to buy his/her producing white or read grpae products to drink.

Hence, in competition psychological view, may influence many New Zealand white or reaad wine producers had been beginning to change their learning behavior on researching what method is the best in order to produce the best quality of taste red or white wine products to sell in order to attract overseas or local white or read grape wine drinkers to choose to buy his/her wine products. Their behavior will focus on learning how to raising or improving white or read grape wine taste method more than only focus on producing a large number white or red grape wine products. They believe wine quality is more important to compare wine producing number. So, New Zealand wine producers themselves wine producers behaviors have been changing on concentrating on researching wine quality method aspect more then wine producing number aspect in behavioral economic view.

America high technological productive behavior

For America example, US is one high technological country, it owns many high technological knowledge talent inventors, e.g. computer science inventors. Hence, US must attract many diferent countries owning high technological computer inventors choose to go to US to develop their computer science profession career. Also, it seems that when many computer science inventors or professions choose to go to US to develop themselves computer science new career. In behavioral economic view, due to their leaving themselves countries choice, which may bring influence themselve country job behaviors need to be changed. They must need to adapt US new live. Because they will forgive their past computer science job. These computer science professionals need to spend time to adapt US new lives. They " past computer science job behaviors" will need to be changed to their new US any computer employer's new computer science job model.

Because their traditional computer science jobs needed to be forgot in their themselves countries. They will feel their old computer science job knowledge and behavior needed to change in order to let their US any one new of computer company employer feels satisfactory to accept their new working behavior in any one US computer organization.

So, on the other hand, many US computer company employer will feel that they must need time to accept any one new overseas computer science professions their working behaviors, their working attitude daily, because these foreign comouter science professional, their past computer working behaviors and working attitude must be different to US domestic computer science professions.

In behavioral economic view, these overseas computer science professions, their working behaviors and attitude must be needed to change in order to adapt any one US new computer company itself domestic or local computer science professional stafs themselves daily working behaviors and attitude because these overseas and local computer science professionals must need to team work together.

In behavioral economic view, it is only one way that foreign computer science professionals must need to change themselves past country traditiona daily working behaviors and attitude in order to cooperate with these US local computer science professionals in teams more easily.

Consequently, if these foreign compute science professionals can change their past working behaviors and attitude to let any one US local computer science professional feels to cooperate with them easily in short time. Then, the US computer company itself whole computer professional teams themselves efficiencies will be influenced to raised or improved by the changing past working attitude and working behaviors of these foreign computer science professionals. So, in behavioral economic view, only if US any one computer company hopes itself computer teams themselves efficiency can be raised or improved when it decides to employ foreign computer science professionals and US domestic computer science professionals. They need to work in teams together. They must need to let these foreign computer science professionals to know how to change their working behaviors and attitude to let their domestic computer science professionals feel easy to work together. Then, the US computer company itself whole team efficiency must be rasied or improved easily in short time.

- China share market investing behavior

For China share market example, economic development depends on financial market. Because if many Chinese have interest to invest to carry on shares buying and selling activities in orde to learn how to earn shares interest and share profit when the China shareholder can make decision to sell himself/herself shares in the the high price, then he/she can earn money when he/she can sell the China company's shares in the high sale share price position.

If China has many Chinese like to spend time to carry on investing shares activities. Themselves shares buying and selling behaviors will influence

China has many companies can increase fund from many Chinese shareholders in order to have enough money to expand or develop themselves businesses in China in long term.

Consequently, when China can have many Chinese like to attempt to carry on buying and selling shares investing behaviors in China share market. Themselves buying and selling shares behaviors can help many Chinese companies have effort to increase enough money or capital in order to continue to do their businesses in long term absolutely. So, it explains why when many Chinese become shareholders , they can assist China will have many companies continue to develop their businesses if many Chinese like to carry on shares buying and selling investing behaviors in long time in China financial investment market nowadays in behavioral economic view.

Why has any individual country have many people invest share behavior which can influence the country's macro consumption desire?

I shall apply shares market buying and selling investment behavior to explaiin why shares investment behavior which may impact the country's overal consumption desire as below:

In behavioral economic view, I assume that when the coutry has many people have interest to attempt to carry on shares buying and selling investment behavior, then their frequent shares buying and selling behaviors which may bring negactive consumption desire or shopping desire of these shares investors their consumer behavior.

The reason is simple, when the country has many share buyers number suddenly been increasing rapidly. Consequently, these large group share investors must need to spend much time to research any kinds of company shares variations, whether when their share prices will rise up of fall down in order to achieve buying the company's shares in the lowest price and selling the company's shares in the highest price level in order to earn profit.

Basic on this reason, they must need to spend much extra time to research share prices changing behavior every day, e.g. one working person will wait to leave his/her job, after he/she can spend time to gather data to research the day's share price changing behavior after dinner. So, the working person's right time may be his/her share price market research behavior. Before he/she may spend his/her night time to go to shopping after dinner, but nowadays, he/she will fogive to do his/her shopping behavior before dinner or after dinner at hight sometime. He/she will make decision to spend much night time to turn on computer to click on share market

website to research his/her share purchase choice to investigate whether his/her share price whether it rises up or falls down at the moment in order to make his/her share buying or selling decision at ever night time.
I mean the when the country has many people are share investors, their shares investment behavioral spenging time which will influence many shops lose customers at might often because the country will have many people feel need to spend night time to turn on computer or watch television to investigate share price variation. So, the country will have many people / share investors choose to stay at home in order to carry on share price variation investigation behavior, they need to listen share market update news from radios or watch the share market update news from computer or TV at home every night. Consequenly, they must reduce times to leave themselves homes at night. So, their shopping behavior also will be reduced. Because these share investors feel need to spend time to investigate share price variation news at homes which can bring economic benefits (high opportunity benefits) when they choose to forgive to leave homes to go to shopping times (opportunity cost) every night.
On conclusion, it seems that when the country has many people are share investors, then their share price investigating behavior may bring negative shopping emotion at night. Consequently, the country's any one shop may lose many customers from this share investor consumer group in behavioral economic view. Hence, when the country's share investors number had been increasing rapidly, it will influence any shops lose many customers from this share investing customer group at night frequenly in short time, even long time in behavioral economic view, because their shopping desires or shopping emotion will be brought negative feeling when they make decisions to spend much time to listen radios or watch TV or computers share price update nes at night. Hence, share market will bring negative impact to influence consumer shopping desire or negative shopping emotion in behavioral economic view.

Can technology influence human shopping behavioral change?
Nowadays, technological development has reached mature stage, whether technological mature stage may bring positive or negative shopping emotion influence to global consumers. I shall aplly internet inventin or ecommerce shopping channel tool to explain whether internet technology can bring postive or negative influence to global consumer behavior in behavioral economic view.

Internet is a good technological tool, it brings e-commerce business chance. In fact, commonly, global has have many businessmen choose to use internet channel to carry on their products transactions between global online-buyers and their electronic websites. So, global many shoppers had begun to feel online shopping is more convenient to compare visiting shops shopping. Their shopping behaviors have been changed from internet technological tool. Global has many shoppers choose to buy any products from any overseas or local businessmen their web stores. They only need to spend time to find any businessmen their webstores to choose the most suitable products to pay visa to buy from their webstores. at homes. So, in general, global had have may shoppers had changed their shopping behaviors from visiting shops to visiting webstores at homes often.

So, it seems that internet technological tool had influenced global many shops disappear, but internet webstores will be replaced their actual shops on streets. Some of businessmen either they choose webstores to replace shops or choose websotes and shops both or still keep shops only. Hence, internet tool influences global businessmen have three kinds of products sale channels to let globa local and overseas consumers to choose how to buy their products.

However, in fact, many of global shoppers, youngers and olders had begun to accept to buy any products from webstores. They feel to spend time to leave homes to visit shops , their shopping behaviors will be wasted time to not essential part to their daily lives. Hence, since internet technological invention, it had changed many consumers their traditional visiting shops shopping habit to change to buying products from webstores channel.

However, on the one hand, internet creates webstores ecommerce shopping channel to let global many consumers do not need to leave homes to go to shopping. It brings negative visiting shops shopping emotion to global general consumers nowadays. But on the other hand, it also brings positive visiting internet webstores shopping emotion to global general consumer nowadays. So, it seems that global many consumers feel that they often do not need to spend much time to go out shopping. Many global consumers feel convenient and enjoy to choose any products to buy from different internet webstores, when the online buyer chooses the most suitable product, he she only needs to pay visa card to buy the product from the online seller's webstore conveniently at home.

Hence, online shopping can bring economic benefit to online buyers, e.g. avoiding walking time or spending transport fare to visit the shop to go to shopping, shortening or reducing shopping time to do another important matter.

On conclusion, global many consumers began feel online shopping can bring more economic benefits on shortening shopping time, avoiding transport fare spending aspect. So, online shopping will be popular shopping behavior for future long time. It may encourage global many shoppers can make rapid shopping decision in short time in order to carry on any products buying transaction to global any one online shopper in short time easily in behavioral economic view. So, global many businessmen had begun to build themselves one attraction webstore in order to persuade different countries consumers to choose to click themselves webstores from internet channel to buy any kinds of products in short time easily.

So, internet technology had changed consumers traditional shopping behaviors to build positive online shopping emotion as well as raise online sellers' any products sale chance easily in behavioral economic view.

Why and how human behavior may influence the country's economic growth or recession?

When one country has many people choose to do the same matter for one period, whether their behavior may influence the country's pvera; economic growth or recession . I shall attempt to indicate cases toexplain their relationship as below:

For flowing rubblish behavioral case example, do you feel that when the country has many people often flow rubblish on the streets, instead of their flowing rubblish behavior may bring streets dirty? But, their flowing rubblish behavior may explain that this country has people may have enough money to buy food to ear, or enough cloths to wear, enough bottles of water to drink, even they may have enough money to buy new television, radio, refrigeraters , washing machines, desktops or laptops electronic home products from old to new to use in order to satisfy their living needs. So, when they flow old electronic home products, their flowing old home electronic products behaviors may seem that they have enough money to buy other new home electronic products to replace old home electronic products to use at homes.

However, it seems thaat this country ought have many people have jobs to do. So, many of them, they can easy to make purchase decison to flow any old home electronic products and buy any new home electronic products to use . Because this country has many people have jobs to do. So, they can often not use old home electonic products to become rubblishs to flow on

streets after they had bought any kinds of new home electronic homes.
In fact, it also implies that this country's economy grows rapidly. So, many businesses can glow up rapdly. When they expanded their businesses, they must need to increase employees number in order to let they help themselves to raise productivity or serve their clients absolutely. So, when the country has many businesses can grow up, it seems that its economy must be better or it is improved to compare past. Due to many different kinds of home electronic products had been often bought to use by this country people in this period. So, this country's any streets can be observed that expensive electronic home products were flowed on streets anywhere. then, this country will have many electronic home products sellers can sell their home electronic products very easily. When this country has many people can find any kinds of jobs to do easily. So, due to unemploymen rate had been decreasing.
In behavioral economic view, as this many electronic home products rubblish country case, we can observe this country may have many people have jobs to do. So, consumption number has been increased long time. So, cheap food, or expensive home electronic products may be rubblish on any streets. This country's people , their flowing rubblish behaviors may be explained that many of people have enough jobs to do, so they have ability to buy any good taste food to eat or buy any kinds of expensive electronic home products to use. So, this country's economy may be improved for this long period. So, in behavioral economic view, when this country can have many electronic home products rubblishs are flowed on anywherer in streets frequently. It seems that this country will have many people have jobs to do, so it causes they often change old home electronic products or replaced them easily, when they have enough income to spend to buy any kinds of new home electronic products to use at homes easily. Moreover, their flowing old electronic home products behaviors also indicate that this country has many people their salaries may be increased in possible from their emplyers. When this country can have many different kinds of home electornic products are sold. It means that this country's electronic home products needs or demand had been increasing, due to many people have jobs to do and income increases to excite their living of needs also improve. Consequently, this country may seem have better economic improvement. We can observe from this country's electronic home products rubblish increasing income in theis period.
On conclusion, this country ought experience economic growth at this

period. So, " flowing expensive electronic home rubblish increasing number " may seem that this country's economic growth is rapidly in this period, due to many people have jobs to do as well as salaries increase in this period.

Technology how impacts human behavior changing?
Technology how influences human behavior to bring changing? For example, online share purchase and sale transaction from smart phone brings share investor can do share buying or selling transation in any where and any time conveniently, non manual driving auto vehicle, bring car owner feels comfortable and spends free time to do other matter, e.g. reading, listening mucis in himself or herself car freely. electrical energy vehicle can help car owner to reduce air polluton and it can brings the drivers do not feel drive long time in any journeys in order to avoid air pollution for environmental protection responsible car drivers in our societies. Thus, they will drive long time in any journeys when they can drive electronic energy cars to replace oil energy cars.
However, online technology can also bring consumers can choose to stay at homes to buy any things from seller individual online webstore conveniently. Such as online technology can bring shoppers do not need to spend much time to visit shops to buy any things. They can choose any kinds of products from any online sellers individual online webstores conveniently at homes. Online technology excite busy consumers can make purchase decision easily as well as it can help online sellers sell any kinds of products from internet easily.
In behavioral economic view, technology can change human behavior to be improved, it can let human feels comfortable, more free time ro use, rapid making any decisions, such as apply smart phones to make share purchase or sale transaction decision, online shopping decision, even travelling any where decision in short time, when the traveller finds the most cheap hotel accommodation room price and air ticket price frm any travel agent online tourism webstore, then the potential travel customer can follow the online hotel accommodation price and air ticket price data to make decision when to buy the air ticket from the airline travel agent or make decision when to prebook which hotel accommodation room to go to the country to travel from online travel agent tourism webstores. So, technology can encourage global any country travelers to make anywhere to trvel rapidly. If the traveler can find the country's general hotel rooms and airline tickets prices had been decreasing more sightly. The traveler may make travel

decision to choose the country to travel in short time, then he/she can prebook the country;s any hotel room and airline ticket to pay by visa fraom the country's any hotel and airline travel agent webstores., before one week, even one month or more easily. Hence, online technology can also encourage traveler individual frequent travel times to be increased, due to global travelers can find any hotel rooms and airline tickets prices from internet conveniently at homes. They do not need to spend time to visit any airline travel agent to enquire travel choice country's hotel rooms prices and airline ticket prices. They can compare global travel of countries choices ' all hotels rooms and airline agents air tickets prices to make prebook airline seat and hotel room decision before one week, one month even six months early.

On conclusion, online technology can encourage global travelers can make travelling any where and when traveling time desicions easily. It can excite tourism industry develops in long time. Also, such as electricity cars invention can encourage environment protection car owners do car purchase decision easily, because they can choose to drive electronic energy cars to replace oil energy cars in order to avoid air pollution occurs easily. So, electronic cars can increase electronic car purchasrs number, due to many of environmental protection attitude of car owners can choose to drive electricity cars to bring air cleans, even non -manual driving cars can encourage lazy driving and free time driving car owners to choose to buy non-manual (artificial intelligent) cars to drive , because they can spend much free time to read, listen music or do any matters in themselves cars, they do not need to drive cars, robotic (AI) auto driving machine is such one non-manual driver to help them to drive themselves cars confidently. So, non-manual driving cars can attract lazy and enjoying free time driving car owners to choose to buy to replace traditional manual cars to drive easily. Moreover, online share transaction can help any share investors to make share buying and selling decision in short time easily. When they can apply smart phones technological tool to carry on share buying and selling activities easily. They can observe any share rising or falling price suitation from smart phones in any where any any time easily. So, smart phone technology can help global any shareholders to make share purchase and sale transaction easily. So, technology can encourage human makes decision in short time rapidly.

How and why employees behaviors may influence economy development?

In behavioral economy view,I believe the country's any organizational employees behavior may bring indirect relationship to influence the country's long term economic development. I shall indicate past manufacture industry social development period to explain their relationship. For many countries' past business activities had belonged to manufacturing industry, such as US, UK past before 1980 year, it focused on steel manufacturing and steel manufacturing related machine products. So, US, Uk developed countries manufacturing industries may be past main country's economic income sources. I assume US , UK past had one million number different kinds of industries. They ought had about seven houndred thousand number organizational businesses were belonged to manufactured industry. They may include:

Steel manufacturing and steel related machine manufacturing, e.g. vehicle manufacturing, home appliances, e.g. washing machine, television, radio, refrigerate cooler, heater, air condition etc. different kinds of different kinds of steel -related manufacturing machine, they were manufactured from US, UK steel machine manufacturers. So, US, Uk the other three hundred thousand number industry may be general service industry, e.g. hotel service, restaurent, cinema, public transport service, tourism lesiure , wine bar, supermarket etc. different kinds of non-manufacturing industries business organizations were operated in UK, US past before 1980 year.

So, in UK, US developed countries industry development history, they ought have high percentage of businesses belonged to steel related manufacturing machine and steel products. Also, in the past before 1980 year, US, Uk business employers , they employed many workers are manufacturing workers. They needed to spend long time to work in factories. They were skillful workers, and they are trained to manufacturing cars, washing machine, television, heater, etc. even steel itself different kinds of steel related products to prepare to deliver to their shops to sell to US, Uk local or overseas clients.

So, I believe that past UK, US ought employ many employees, they belonged to skillful manufacturing workers, manufacture increasing steel machine or steel related machine number of products rapidly daily. So, if UK, US had had many of these manufacturing factories owned high skillful workers, then their manufacturing steel-related machine or steel both kinds of products number must be influenced to raise rapidly. Consequently, their steel machine manufacturing products would been exported to overseas or would been sold to local both markets , they may be influenced to raise sale number. They (these manufacturing workers) needed to be trained to know how to manufactur these different kinds of machine products in the efficient teams and they ought to be trained to raise their efficiencies in order to shorten time to manufacturing many kinds of steel related manufacturing machine or steel itself products rapidly. So , if their efficiencies and manufacturing performance was improved, these US, UK any one manufacturing worker and their teams ought achieve raising productivities significantly.

Hence, when past UK, US manufacturing industry development period, if these two countries‘ any manufacturing factories could have many manufacturing workers could be trained to be skillful and proficient manufacturing workers. Then, in past every day to these factories workers, they ought help their steel or steel related manufacturing employers to raise any kinds of machine or steel products number in every team. So, when past in the manufacturing industry development, US, UK could have many factories' manufacturing workers themselves steel or steel related machine products manufacturing skill could be trained to to improve to any kinds of these machine or steel manufacuring products quality as well as their products number could be influenced to raise by themselves skillful improvement significantly every day.

Then, what would be influenced to occur to past UK, US manufacturing industry period? In behavioral economic view, when these two manufacturing industry developed countries, such as UK, US , if they had many factories workers can be trained to improve their skill in order to achieve any kinds of steel or steel-related machine products quality could be improved as well as products manufacturing number could be also increased absolutely.

In consequence, past UK and US both countries ought increase themselves any kinds of steel and steel related machine products number to be supplied to themselves local shops to let local clients to choose any one kind of machine manufacturing products to buy easily as well as they could also export to supply overseas any countries to buy their different kinds of steel or steel related machine products to let overseas steel or steel related manufacturing machine product buyers, they can have many of these different kinds of these steel or steel-related different kinds of manufacturing machine from UK and UK these both countries easily to compare other countries.

On conclusion, I believe that past US, and UK macro manufacturing industry income GDP would increase significantly. So, they would have good economic growth performance because when many of these manufacturing workers themselves manufacturing effort could be improved. So, it explained when employees manufacturing abilities can influence economic growth indirectly.

Robots invention whether they can help organizations to raise efficiencies or inefficiencies?

In behavioral economic view, in any organizations, when the organization hopes its worker teams can raise efficiencies , the organization may choose to increase more workers number and/or it can provide training to improve these workets themselves skills in order to raise their efficiencies. For one warehouse example, when the warehouse increases many goods , they are needed to delivered these goods from the shelves to the delivering destination locations. If this warehouse supervisors feel these workers themselves goods delivery speeds are slow, which is possible due to this warehouse's workers number is not enough. So, this warehouse supervisor ought increase workers number in order to increase their goods delivery speed in order to deliver goods from the shelves to every indicated goods delivery destination in order to let any one lorry driver can transport the right kinds of goods and ensure the accurate goods number to transport to any one client home rapidly.

However, if this warehouse supervisor planed to buy several warehouse goods delivery robots to assist these warehouse workers to find the right kinds of goods from shelves and then deliver to the right destination location in the warehouse. So, these warehouse orkers can concentrate on counting the accurate goods number and ensuring the right kinds of goods in order to prepare to let lorry drivers to transport these goods to these goods of buyers themselvers homes rapidly. Consequently, in the first step, robots can concentrate on finding th right goods from shelves and delivers them to the right goods transportation of location destination. Then, in the second step, these warehouse workers can concentrate on counting the accurate goods number and ensuring the right kinds of goods in order to prepare to put them to the lorry. Consequently, when warehouse robots and warehouse workers can cooperate to work together, the most important, robots, can deal on finding the right kinds of goods and deal on delivering the accurate number of goods of job duty as well as these warehouse workers can only concentrte on counting the right kinds of goods number in order to avoid it has none any mistake of wrong kinds of goods and inaccurate goods of delivery number to be transported to the lorry and to deliver to any one buyer's home.

So, it seems that warehouse robots ought help any one warehouse worker to raise himself efficiency and avoid goods delivery of mistake occurrence easily as well as their help to warehouse workers that can let any one goods buyer feels their goods can be delivered to their homes rapidly. Moreover, warehouse robots can also help these warehouse workers to raise efficiencies because warehouse robots can help them to shorten goods delivery time between any one shelf and any one goods delivery destination of location in the warehuse because robots may help them to find the right kinds of goods from the right shelf in the short time. So, any one worker does not need to spend long time to seek anywhere is the right shelf location for the kind of goods when the kind of goods are needed to deliver to the buyer's home from lorry. Warehouse robots can help them to do this aspect of " finding the goods from the right shelf in short time job duty". So, any one warehouse worker only needed tospend less time to do the counting of any right kind of goods number and ensuring the right kind of goods job duty. Consequently, this warehouse 's any one worker, his any one kind of goods delivery time may be reduced, because robots' assistance and they may have more confidence to avoid mistake to deliver the wrong number of goods and/or the wrong kind of goods to any one goods buyer's home.

On conclusion, it seems that warehouse robots ought may help any one warehouse worker to raise efficiency for any one team in the warehouse as well as the warehouse any one supervisor does not need to spend much time to observe any one worker individual performance for " goods delivery job duty aspect" because their goods delivery job duty that had been replaced to do by these several warehouse robots. Robots can achieve the more accurate of right kinds of goods and the right number of goods delviery job performance to compare any one of human warehouse worker themselves right kinds of goods of delivery and right number of goods of delivery job performance. So, when robots can participate to cooperate with this warehouse's any one worker to do their goods of delivery job duty in this warehouse every day. Then, robots can raies any one of supervisor individual confidence in order to let they do not need to spend time to observe any one of worker individual whose goods of delivery job performane. They can concentrate on supervising any one worker whose goods transport to lorry in the final step in order to avoid to deliver wrong goods number and / or wrong kind of goods to any one goods buyer's home every day. Consequently, this warehouse's overall teams of their delviery of goods performance many be improved by robotss' participatin to goods of delivery task as well as this warehouse's oveall teams themselves efficiencies may be influenced to raise by robots' goods of delivery task participation.

Why social behavior may influence organizational strategy needs to be changed ?

Why any organizations need to know whether nowadays social behaivor how has been changing in order to implement the kind of the most right strategy to achieve the profit aim pursue in possible. I shall indicate nowadays ecommerce or online, customer shopping behavior to explain above question concerns they ought have close relationship between social behavior and organizational strategic choice or organizational behavioral changing need.

On nowadays ecommerce business, or online shopping model, this kind of shopping model in global many young and old age consumers like to apply internet tool to choose any country sellers website stores in order to stay at home to buy any kinds of products from themselves webstores in global societies.

In fact, online shopping model had been popular for long time above to twenty years. Most of global sellers will make decision to design themselves webstores in order to attract global many online buyers to choose to buy their products from themselves webstores. So, it seems that social consumers purchase behaviors had been changed to online shopping from internet invention.

Hence, social consumers purchase behavioral changes may influence any organizations' strategies need to be changed from visiting shops purchase strategy model to online purchase strategy model, if the seller still concentrate on concentrate on considerate how to design itelf , but neglects to considerate how to design itself webstore, e.g. how to design attract product photos to put on itself webstore, how to arrange sale price information location to be putted on webstore and visa card payment location on itself webstore in order to let any one online buyer can feel very easier to buy itself any kinds of products from itself webstore. Then, its potential online buyers will be influenced to increase number when they can find this online seller itself any kinds of products photes and every kinds of product sale price information and visa card payment channel locations easily from itself webstore.

So, it implies that nowadays any one seller ought need to design one webstore to let any one online overseas and domestic consumers can have chance to click itself webstore to choose any one kind of product to buy conveniently when he/she does not hope to leave him/her home to go to shop, because nowadays social shopping behaviors had been influenced to change when internet invention, them it gives another online purchase method to replace visiting shops purchase method to global any one buyer in nowadays societies.

So, if nowadays any one seller still concentrate on how to design itself shop display in order to put any kinds of product on shelf in order to let any one visiting shop customer to find the kind of product to buy, but it neglects to change to choose to pursue another new technological shopping method, such as webstore purchase method in order to implement effective strategy to design the most right webstore as well as in order to attract global overseas and local consumers to find itself webstore easily from website and find its any one kind of product phots and sale price and visa card payment button in order to choose to buy itself any kinds of products in the short time. Consequently I believe that the seller will lose many customers from overseas and local when its other same or similar product sellers choose to design themselves webstores in order to let global any one product buyer can buy themselves any one kind of product when they can pay visa card to buy their products from them webstores conveniently when they stay at home habitly. Then, the seller will lose many global potential customers in long time.

On conclusion, in behavioral economic view, any consumer behavioral social changing, which will influence any in order to avoid customers number loses significantly . In future time, organizations need to make rapid decision in order to implement the most reasonable and the most useful strategy in order to avoid global potential customers number reduces or lose them in long time. So, social behavioral changing environment ought influence any global organizations need to decide how to change themselves strategies in order to avoid customers loses significantly in future time.

How and why human behavior may influence economic growth or recession?

May ourselves daily behaviors influence our global societial continue economic growth or recession? Do they have cause and effect close relationship between human behaviors and global economic growth or recession? I shall apply behavioral economic theory to analyze and explain whether ourselves daily behaviors and our global societial economic growth or recession which have close cause and effect relationship as below:

Every country itself economic development must depend on any business activities, otherwise, any kinds of business activities must need ourselves business activities or behaviors in order to achieve any business activities as well as achieve the country's overall economic development in macro view. However, any country's overall business activites or behaviors which must depend on any kinds of individual businessmen, themselves employees daily working behavior or activity or performance in order to help them to attract or increase many clients number to acieve " earning profit" aim. So, it seems that any individual business, itself overall every department individual working behavior is one main factor to influence the company's overall business performance.

For agricultural fruit and meat food farming industry example, such as New Zealand is a farming main target industry country. It had had many New Zealanders were daily themselves own farming businesses for many years. Their farming businesses include growing fruit, sheep, cow, pig pork, meat etc. food sale business. If the New Zealand farmer owned a large size farming land, then he will choose either growing fruit or feeding sheeps, pigs, cows to be meat to to transport to New Zealand supermarkets to help them to sell to their farmers meet to New Zealanders in order to earn profit. Thus, if the New Zealand farmer owned large size of farming lands, then he needs to employ many farming employees (farming workers) to help him to carry on farming business daily tasks, e.g. picking up friuts, feeding pigs, cows, sheeps to eat food daily. These daily farming jobs are very important to influence this New Zealand farmer's meats or fruits sale number whether they can be easy or diffcult to sell in New Zealand supermarkets , if these farming workers can own encough farming knowledge or skill to know how to pick up fruits method and make judgement to know whether it is right time to pick up the kind of fruits from the trees , as well as know how feed this pigs, sheeps, cows to eat food in order to let they are better health. Consequently, their farming behaviors which can let these animals can provide the best taste and enough meat from these animals to let New Zealander to buy to eat from New Zealand any one supermarket. Even these New Zealand farming workers can know whether the kinds of fruits, e.g. oranges, apples, gapes etc. fruits whether they ought be picked up from the trees at the right time. Consequently, they can make judgement to decide to pick up any kinds of the best taste fruits to let any one New Zealander to buy to eat from any one supermarket in New Zealand. Otherwise, if they do not make judegement to know whether the kind of fruit ought not be picked up because they still need longer time to continue grow up to increase fruit size and better taste from the trees in order to let any one fruit buyer can feel better taste when they eat this kind of fruit later. If they can buy this kind of fruit to eat later, then this New Zealand farmer's his fruit buyers can buy the best taste of this kind of fruit to eat from an yone supermarket in New Zealand. Consequently, many New Zealand supermarkets will choose to buy any kinds of fruits from this farmer fruit supplier when they feel this farmer's fruits can provide more better taste fruits to compare other farmers‘ fruits.

Thus, due to New Zealand is one farming main income source country. It's any kinds of fruits and meats need to be export to overseas to sell , instead of local sale. It's GDP percent is very high to whole country 's overall income source. So, any one New Zealand farmer individual and any one farming worker individual working behavior will influence its economy whether it is influenced to grow or recession possible. Moreover, it also seems that farming workers' farming knowledge and skill will influence themselves farming daily activities to achieve the aim of the number of increase or decrease to any kinds of fruits whether they are better taste or the number of increase of decrease to any kinds of meats whether they are better taste to supply to any one New Zealand fruit or meat buyers to eat from any one New Zealand supermarket. So, it implies that any one New Zealand farming worker individual farming behavior may influence any kinds of fruits or any kinds of meat taste because they are transported to any one supermarket to sell in New Zealand.

Consequently, if New Zealans had many farmers can teach god farming knowledge and skill to let their any one farming workers know how to decide judgement to decide when it is right time to pick up any kinds of fruits from trees , or how to grow them on soil in order to let they can grow rapidly. Then, many different kinds of fruits can be provided to let any one New Zealanders can eat the best taste of fruits when their fruits are supplied to any one New Zealand supermarkets. Even, if they knew how to feed foods to pigs, cows, sheeps to eat daily. Then they can be more health and they can provide the best taste of meats to let any one New Zealanders can buy their meats from any one New Zealand supermarkets. Moreover, their fruits and meats can be transported to overseas to let any one country fruits or meats buyers can choose any kinds of New Zealand meats and fruits to buy to eat from themselves countries supermarkets. Then, many overseas fruit and meat buyers will perfer to choose New Zealand any kinds of fruits or meats to buy to compare other countries fruits or meats to buy when they go to any one local supermarkets.

On conclusion, it seems that New Zealand farming workers themselves farming behavior may influence their farming employers any kinds of fruits or meats sale number and income because their farming task behaviors must influence whether their fruits or meats taste are the better taste or worse taste to compare their other local farmers (the farmer competitors) whose fruits or meats taste. If tthe farmer's any one farming worker can be trained to learn how to know to feed animals skill and when is the most right time to pick up any kinds of fruits from trees or how to grow them on the soil methods. Due to these farming worker individual farming behavior may influence his different finds of fruits and meats sale number to be increase or decrease, so these any one New Zealand farmer must need to depend on any one farming worker whose farming working methods, if their farming working behaviors can be the best to influence any kinds of fruits to grow rapid or any kinds of pigs, cows, sheeps animals grow up rapidly , then their sale number may be increase significantly and their taste can be improved to let any New Zealand or overseas meat or fruit buyer to buy to eat to feel from any one New Zealand or overseas supermarkets, then New Zealand's agriculture industry must be influenced to increase. In the world, any one fruit or meat buyer must choose to buy New Zealand's fruit and meat to eat in prefer to compare other countries' fruits and meats. So, New Zealand's GDP may be influenced to raise from any one New Zealand farming worker individual farming working behaviors.

Reasons why human behavior may influence economic recession or growth?

Can ourselves daily behaviors or activies influence ourselves countries' economic growth or recession? I shall attempt to explain the reasons why they have direct or indirect relationship between human behavior and economy growth or recession as below:

I shall indicate environment pollution case to attempt to explain above question. Our societies had been experiencing servious environment pollution challenge. However, environment pollution , such as air pollution is caused by air planes and vehicles emission by air planes and vehicles emission as well as water pollution is caused by plastic rubblish, or dirty water or oil or gas chemical material, these both kinds of pollution ought may bring economic recession and this both kinds of pollution are caused by human ourselves daily foolish activities.

I believe human behavior and economy and pollution which have cause and effect relationship. I shall analyze this environment pollution case to explain why they have case and effect relationship between human foolish behavior and environment pollution and economic recession as below:

When global societies had many people like to buy cars to drive to bring emission to fresh air on the roads as well as many manufacturing factories will bring emission to pollute fresh air in their manufacturing processes. Factories and cars will bring air pollution , due to factories need to pollute fresh air in order to manufacture many products and car owners need to drive their cars to go to offices or leisure places. Their cars will also bring emisson to pollute fresh air. On consequence, car owners themselves frequent driving behaviors and factory workers themselves frequent manufacturing behaviors may bring environment pollution. Technology or human behavior whether may influence economic growth or recession. Moreover, air planes also brings emission to pollute air when they are flying in sky. Also, when ships bring oil pollution or sea plastic rubblishs bring pollution to global oceans.

In fact, manufactuers and cars owners, such as factories workers manufacturing behaviours ans car owners driving behaviors and pilots driving air planes flying behaviors and ships transport behaviors, which may cause plastic rubblish, oil or gas emission to sky or sea or on the road to cause ocean and air pollution is serious. However, human ourselves need to buy cars to drive to satisfy ourselves driving leisure or enjoyment, travelers need to catch air planes to travel to enjoy leisure needs, factories workers need help factories to manufacture many products to sell to customers to satisfy their using needs. oil exploration needs to find lands to explore new oil lands.

All of these business and leisure activites may bring serious air and water pollution. However, due to serious air and water pollution will bring earth warming challenge , such as some countries temperature will be influences to rise up to 40 degree or higher br earth warming. However, earth warming is caused by air and ocean pollution. Pollution must be caused by human ourselves, driving cars leisure and factories manufacturing business activities. Hence, if human decided to continue to do these foolish behaviors, we only pursue to manufacture different kinds of industrial products or drive cars to enjoy leisure aims, but we also neglect ourselves behaviors may bring environment pollution. Then, earth warming or earth temperature will be influenced to rise up absolutely in long term. Moreover, if our future earth will be influenced to bring serious high temperature effect by human ourselves these foolish behaviors.

On consequencey, warth warming will bring serious economic losses in possible because when ourselves earth temperature had been influenced to rise up to 40 degree or high. Ourselves health will be caused poor, due to we will feel difficult breath, we must need often tried and hard to work, due to our nervous and health will be influenced to poor by pollution and earth warming effect. Also, we need to pay more money to see doctors when we had long life. Then, our societies will lose may strong labors to help manufacturers to work, e.g. factories will reduce workers number to help manufacturers to produce more different kinds of products, due to workers health is general poor. Due to lacking enough workers to manufacture products, our societies will begin to reduce enough supply number of products to sell to global consumers to satisfy their use needs.

On conclusion, in behaviroal economic view, our societies will lose many labors due to their bodies are not health by air and water pollution. Global economic and business activities will be influenced to worse by global workers reducing number reason. So, economic recession will begin to occur in possible when pollution reaches the serious level.

How employee behavior influences organizational development?

Can any organizational department employee individual behavior may help the organization to bring long term development? When one employee individual behavior, manager won't feel whose task behavior may help organizational development, but when the department has many teams cooperate to work together , all of these team employees whose task behaviors may help their organization to bring long term development.

I shall explain how any why when the organization has many departments, as well as when every team memmber individual behavior may help whole organization to bring long term development in possible as below:

Every organization must need efficient department to cooperate to work together. They may include human resource, finance, logistic, facility management, sales, marketing , operateional , warehouse , factory manufacture , research and development, purchase, customer service etc. different kinds of departments to cooperate to work together. So, any one employee individual behavior, include manager, leader, supervisor, worker, salesperson, manufacture worker, adminisration staff, factory or logistic worker etc. themselves task behavior whether his/her performance is worse or better , whose task behavior ought bring long term good or bad influence to cause the organization's whose efficiency, or performance , whether it can be influenced to improve significantly. For car factory manufacture workers department example, it exmploys 100 car manufacturing workers. They need to manufacture at least 50 cars in order to bring enough car manufacture number to supply to global car buyers to choose to buy (satisfaction to car buyers their driving leisure activity needs). However, if this car manufacture firm employs many low skilful car manufacture workers, their inefficient car skill may bring cars manufacture number reduces, they can not achieve to reach the at least 50 cars manufacture number, if these 100 car manufacture workers. They have half number of workers, they only manufacture 30 to 40 cars number at least daily. So, it seems that this car manufacture firm will have half car manufacture workers bring the low cars manufacture number to compare the another half cars manufacture workers, when this proficient car manufacture workers may manufacture at least 60 or more cars manufacture number daily. So, it explains that this inefficient car manufacture workers will not help this car manufacture company to manufacture enough cars number in order to supply to global car market to sell to satisfy global car buyers needs, when car buyers demand number is more thn car manufacture supply number in supply and demand view. Hence, in long term, if this car manufacture company can not employ new proficient car manufacture workers to replace those inefficient or low skillful car workers. Consequently, its car manufacture number must be influenced to reduce and it can not satisfy global car buyers driving leisure needs.

However, if this car manufacture firm also has shop to sell itself any kinds of cars, instead of manufacturing cars product. So, it needs have both main departments to help it to earn profit. The first step, it needs have proficient car manufacture workers to help it to manufacture at least 50 cars from every car worker in order to have enough cars number to be provided to global car sellers to help it to sell to global car customers. Second step, if it decided to attempt to sell itself cars. Then, it needs to set up car shops in global to different countries in order to let global car buyers may visit its global any one car shop to enquire any one car etc. salesperson about any car quality, speed, gas useful, price, safety, etc. information questions and they can attempt to sit in any one car to feel whether which car can let them to feel more comfortable to make final car purchase decision in any one shop. So, if this car company can provide good sale speaking skillful training to any one car salesperson to let his/her to know whether how to explain every kind of car function and feature, manufacture method etc. questions, then I believe that they can influence any one car buyer to makecar purchase choice decision more easily. So, it this car manufacturer hopes it may attempt to earn profit from different countries car sellers and car buyers both. It ought also provide training course to all general car salespeople to be proficient owning sale speaking skillful professional skill in order to prepare having more confidence to persuade any one car customer to make car purchase choice from any one car salesperson more easily to compare global other car sellers.

Hence, if this car manufacturer could build both car manufacturing team and car sale team more proficient. However, if this car manufacturer hopes to develop itself car manufacture busness to expend to car sale business both in success. It must need to spend long term to provide training courses to general car manufacture workers and general car salespeople both to be proficient car skillful manufacture workers and proficient car skillful salespeople in order to help they can manufacture enough car numbers and help they can persuade may car customers can make car purchase decision in short time when they visit its any one car shop.

However, this car manufacture company explains why every car manufacture worker whose manufacturing behavior and every car salesperson sale persuading speaking ability may help this car manufacture company to expand from its car manufacture market to car sale market development in sussess in possible. So, this car manufacture firm must need these two kinds of essential human resource elements in order to achieve its cars sale number and cars manufacture number increasing aim. They may include proficient car manufacture workers and proficient car salespeople both human resource elements. These both human resource daily task behavior may influence its long term task efficient performance in order to expand itself car sale business in success from itself car manufacture business easily. If it hopes to expand its car manufacture business to car sale business in success. It must need to provide training to these two departments general staffs to be proficient staffs in order to supply enough cars number to its global car shops to let global car buyers can choose its any kinds of cars to buy in any time.

Morevoer, if this car manufacture company can have good skillful of car research and development department , it aims to research and innovate any new technological cars invention in order to improve its any traditional old kinds of cars to be innovative new kinds of cars from every year. Consequently, its any new innovative cars ought attract global any one car buyer to make car purchase choice final decision more easily, because its any kinds of manufacturng cars can be innovated rapidly to compare its any one car manufacturing competitors, when its nay kinds of cars can be shorten time to innovate within three months, but its any one car manufacturing competitors need to spend more than three months, even one year to innovate themselves traditional old cars products in long term.

Hence, its car staffs research and development department staffs must need own good car product design ability, proficient car engineering knowledge , even car invention knowledge in order to innovate its any one kind of car product in short time and introduce to let its global car proficient car buyers feel surprise to its any one kind of innovative car products to compare its any one car manufacturer.Hence, these four departments: car manufacture, car sale and car research and development anr car training departments must need concentrate resource to provide enough training to any one staffs in order to achieve the best performance.

On conclusion, all these departments staffs their performance can influence car manufacture aim to chance to car manufacture and sale aim more significantly. it explains why some main department staffs whole behaviors may influence any organizational performance significantly.

Artificial intelligent Human clever and art creating ability methods

How robots create human clever and art creating ability? Nowadays robots invention may help businesses to reduce employees number, improve performance, raise productivities, reduce cost in service industry,manufacturing industry, office , warehouse, restaurant, hotel , factory, cinema etc. different kinds of business environments, even public transport tools. However, instead of robots may bring these above advantages to any kinds of business working and service environments, whether robots may also help human to create clever and image creating ability. I shall attempt to answer this question:

On the one hand, I believe that past technology ,e.g. machine , it should not have ability to help human to create clever and image creative ability,but nowadays, robots invention that I believe it had had enough ability to help future human to raise more clever and more creating image or painting picture, art design etr. image ability, after robots had been experienced above more than ten years improvement stage from early research stage to invention stage, till to nowadays improvement stage, e.g. non-manual driving auto vehicels, even future non-manual driving skill may be improved to apply to public transport tools, e.g. trams, trains,buses, airplanes, ships etc. public transport tools, when non-manual driving skills can be improved to own the most safe driving skillful ability to compare human driving skills.

On another hand, when robots could be invented to be applied to medical or hospital surgery aspect, e.g. roboting surgerys may help surgery doctors to do complex surgery in surgery rooms, or serving patients tasks in any hospital working environments. They can help nurses and doctors to spend more time to do more important tasks urgently, so medical or surgery serving robots may help nurses and surgery doctors to reduce task load pressure and create clever or improve their surgery skills to when they can cooperate to work in hospitals.

On the other hand, robots can be invented to help any public transport drivers to avoid more traffic accidents occurrence on any countries roads. So, it seems that non-manual driving public transport tools invention may also help human drivers to improve driving skills in possible, when they can learn how to avoid sudden traffic accidents occurrence in any countries roads in any time. so, any kindsof public transport tool drivers ought learn how to avoid traffic accidents skills from future non-manual driving robots invention. Instead of non-manual driving robots and hospital patients medical care or surgery service robots may help public transport tools drivers and hospital nurses and doctors to concentrate on spending time to treat any more important and urgent matters every days. Even, future restaurants may let cooking restaurants may let cooking robots to help human cookers to cook more different kinds of good taste food, to human cookers may learn cooking robots cooking skills in order to improve themselves traditional cooking skills often, in order to compare their cooking skills between human cookers and cooking robots.

On conclusion, it seems that cooking robots ought help human cookers to create any kinds of new cooking skills. Moremove, futuer robot cookers ought be future human cookers their cooking coaches. These robot cookers will help human cookers to create clever cooking skills in possible. Also, future non-manual driving robots ought help human drivers to create new driving skills in order to improve their driving skills to reduce sudden traffic accidents occurrence easily on any countries roads in any time, future hospital surgery or patient care service robots may help surgeons or nurses to do any surgerys in surgery rooms or looking care patients in hospitals. So, when robot surgeons help human surgeons to do complex surgerys in surgerical rooms, human surgeons can learn how to do more complex surgerical tasks for every surgeons when human surgeons can observate every surgerical robots how to do surgeons together. Hence, it seems that robot surgeons also may create future human surgeons themselves innovate surgerical skills from traditional surgerical skills improvement. So, future artificial intelligent technology ought help any kinds of human occupations to create clever, even improvement themselves traditional skills to new innovative skills absolutely.

Why does technology raise online products sale demand and reduces shops products sale demand?

Nowadays robot technology is popular to be applied to different aspects of our daily lives. They may include: non-manual driving vehicles, smart phones, space rockets, kitchen cookers, shopping centres service, cinema ticket sale, etc. different kinds of businesses demand. However, instead of internet invention may influence global communication, media channel is changed to computer internet, media channel is changed to computer internet, media communication from traditional newspaper, letter, TV, radio etc. communication channel. So, any internet users may click to yahoo.com news website to read global news from computer yahoo.com website easily.

In fact, internet technology is also used from businesses. They attempt to set up themselves web stores to sell their products from themselves webstores. So, any one product buyers may buy any kinds of products from any one webstores when they stay at homes. It is very convenient and common to future any one webstore shoppers. It brings this question: Can webstores help online product purchases needs raise and influence shop product purchases need reduce?

In demand and supply view, when one product price raises, its sale demand ought reduce, unless, it can attract to influence customers need consideration or its supply number decreases. But, when one product is increasing sale price to seel from the seller's webstore, whether its sale number will be influenced to reduce. Also, when the kind of product is selling and its sale price is raised, whether it can still keep demand number increase as well as whether it can influence its similar kinds of competitor their products sale demand number to reduce from shop sale channel.

In demand and supply view, when one product price raises, its sale demand ought reduce, unless, it can attract to influence customers need consideration or its supply number decreases. But when one product is increasing sale price to sell from the seller's webstore, whether its sale number will be influenced to reduce. Also, when the kind of product is selling and its sale price is raised, whether it can still keep demand number increases as well as whether it can influence its similar kinds of competitors their products sale demand number to reduce from shop sale channel.

I suppose that webstore sale may influence shop sale demand number decreases, because when internet is popular to use, when one country's buyer wants to buy one kind of product, but he/she can not find the kind of product can be bought from himself/herself home country. If he/she can findthe kind of product to buy from any one of overseas webstore from internet channel at home in any time. Then, he/she will be influenced to make purchase decision from the seller's websote immediately. So, it implies that when on consumer plans to buy one kind of product, he / she will attempt to find the kind of product from any one seller's webstore in preferat home, if he/she spend long time to find the kind of product from many of webstores, but he /she still does not find the kind of product from many of webstores, then he/she will choose to visit any one shop to attempt to buy the kind of product.Hence, online shopping purchase channel will be prefer choice to compare visiting shopd purchase channel in nowadays society.

So, it explains that why the kind of product online sale number may influence the kind of similar product visiting shop sale number either increases or decreases. It means that the kind of product visiting shops sale number may still increases , if the kind of similar products supply number is not enough , they are difficult to let any one online buyer to find to buy from any one webstore. Otherwise, if the kind of similar products sale supply number is enough to let any one online buyer to find from many webstores. Then, they can influence the similar kinds of shop products purchase demand to reduce and their shops purchase demand will be also influenced to reduce from webstores purchase channel.

On conclusion, it explains that the kind of shop products demand number ought be influenced to increase or decrease, when the similar kind of products can be bought easily from many webstores from internet (ecommerce) shopping channel. Internet (online) technology may help the seller to raise the kind of product competitive ability on purchase demand aspect, when there are not many other sellers can provide webstores to sell the similar kind of products and they only concentrate on selling the kind of similar products from shops to let any one online buyer to frind from may webstores. Then, they can influence the similar kinds of shop products purchase demand to reduce and their shops purchase demand will be also influenced to reduce from webstores purchase channel. Hence, webstore and shop both purchase channel explains that the similar kinds of shop products demand number will be influenced to increase or decrease , when the kinds of product can be bought easily from many webstores from internet shopping channel. Internet technology may help the seller to raise the kind of product competitive abilty to raise purchase demand when there are not many other sellers can provide webstores to sell the kind of similar products and they only concentrate on selling the kind of similar products from shops.

Does car technological development reach mature stage to help economic development?

Our societies had been developing too many years. In our past technological aspect, machine invention had began till to computer invention till to internet invention. It seems that our technological development stage may reach mature stage. Why do I feel our technological development had reached mature stage. I shall apply demand and supply economic theory to explain this question as below:

I shall indicate car development industry to explain whether when car development stage can reach mature stage, it may help global economic growth. In our car technological development stage, it is from gas energy car invention till to nowadays battery energy car invention till to even future non-manual driving car invention. Do you feel that when human (car buyers) felt environmental protecion need to avoid air pollution. So, battery energy cars demand number may increase , it will influence gas energy cars demand number reduces. Even, if future non0manula driving cars invention succeed, lazy driving car buyers will choose to buy non-manual driving (robot driving cars) in preference. So, it is possible that , it will influence future gas energy cars demand number reduces much. I mean that when car buyers can choose many different kinds of non-manual driving cars and battery energy cars to buy. Then, gas energy cars demand number must be influenced to reduce very much as well as gas energy cars supply number will be influenced to reduce to avoid sale prices reduce.

Hence, it explains why future car technological development will reach mature stage when both kinds of non-manual driving cars and battery energy cars are invented to the mature stage. When these two kinds of cars invention can satisfy future global car buyers driving needs. Then, car maufacturers won't need to spend too much time to continue to attempt to invent any new kinds of cars in order to excite future car buyers' purchase decision. So, I believe that car technological development will reach mature stage within five years, if non-manual driving cars and battery energy cars are invented in success and they can be popular to accept to drive to global car buyers.

On conclusion, when car technological development reaches matural stage, it will help future economy continue grows because when car manufacturers had invented many new kinds of non-manual driving cars and new kinds of non-manual driving cars and new battery energy car sale market. Then, they will encourage or attract global many car buyers choose to buy these both kinds of cars products in preference to compare to traditional gas energy car products. So, they will influence many traditional gas- energy car buyers forgive to drive gas energy cars to avoid non pollution and lazy driving behavioral feeling. So, gas energy car reselling number will increase between gas energy car drivers and past non-owning any car buyers. Also, non-manual driving cars and battery energy car supplying number will be influenced to increase when battery energy car buyers and non-manual driving car buyers driving needs increase.

Consequently, these factors will influence global gas energy cars, non-manual driving cars and battery energy cars their cars purchase and sale transactions increase in future global car market. So, I believe that global car technological development could reach matural stage, then it will infuence global car buyers number increases as well as this car technological mature development stage may also bring global rapid economic growth future non-manual driving car buyers and battery energy car buyers both number increases.

CHAPTER FIVE

Space tourism how influence travel industry employees number reduce

How can psychology method predict space tourism leisure desire? I believe that it has relationship between the space tourism planner and the economic environment as well as his/her psychology as below:

Firstly, on the economic environment influence hand, it includs these both economic situations, either in the good economic environment, many people can earn high income and employers can supply many job number to provide to many people to work, then it will influence the space travelling planner has more space travelling desire. Otherwise, or in the bad economic, less people can earn high income and employers can not supply many job number to provide to many people to work, it will influence the space travelling planner has less space travelling desire.

Secondly, on these both the space travelling planner individual psychology influence hand, the space travelling planner will have these both aspects of individual psychological influence, it includes these both either positive or negative psychological influence aspectsas below:

On the positive psychological influence aspect, if the space travelling planner has confidence to the space travelling leisure company can provide safe, comfortable, good quality of one space travelling trip arrangement, good taste food arrangement, reasonable space ticket price and every reasonable space trip for space hotel living arrangement and space garden and space farming land visiting journey arrangement, even, space swimming pool and space sport centre and space cinema leisure arrangement to let whom to stay on the planet at least one day trip, it means not one short time space trip, e.g. the spacecraft only flies about half hour or one half. It can not fly to the planet to arrive its space station destination to stay to let the space travelling planner to live at the space hotel at least one night. Then the space travelling planner will have more desire to choose to catch the space tourism leisure company's spacecraft to travel to space.

Otherwise, on the negative psychological influence aspect, if the space travelling planner lacks confidence to the space travelling leisure company can provide safe, comfortable, good quality of one space travelling trip arrangement, good taste food arrangement, reasonable space ticket price and every reasonable space trip for space hotel living arrangement and space garden and space farming land visiting journey arrangement, even, space swimming pool and space sport centre and space cinema leisure arrangement to let whom to stay on the planet at least one day trip, it means not one short time space trip, e.g. the spacecraft only flies about half hour or one half. It can not fly to the planet to arrive its space station destination to stay to let the space travelling planner to live at the space hotel at least one night. Then the space travelling planner will have less desire to choose to catch the space tourism leisure company's spacecraft to travel to space.

Hence, it seems economic environment changing factor and the space travelling planner's confidence factor to the space tourism leisure providers will influence the whole space travelling market whose space travelling consumer's space travelling leisure consumption desire to be more or less. So, any one space tourism provider can not neglect these both factors how to influence whose customer consumption desire.

● space tourism strategy

Future any space tourism leisure business needs have good business plan to outline the space tourism leisure business in these aspects , such as: different space tourism destinations of every space tourism journey, technical , financial and regulatory factors for growing space tourism leisure consumption into any one kind of unique artificial intelligent space tourism journey for identified passenger target group.

All how to design one space tourism business development plan to attempt to predict whether what trends will influence how every different kinds of identified space tourism journey in order to achieve passenger number growing aim as well as how to achieve one attractive space tourism leisure to satisfy future space tourism passenger individual space travel needs more easily.

I shall indicate what aspects to future every space tourism traveler who will consider in order to reduce the space tourism traveler personal worry to catch any pace boats to leave our Earth to fly to other planets to travel.

I recommend that any space tourism leisure organizations need to concern these aspects in their space tourism leisure business plan as below:

(1) safe space tourism journey

On first aspect concerns safe space tourism journey plan to let all space tourism travelers will considerate safe issue. They must ensure space boats that is safe to catch them to fly to planets in their space journeys. So, any space tourism leisure business will utilize previous flight rated and proven technologies to form the basis for manufacturing spacecraft vehicles, and will incorporate the latest modern avionics and flight systems for ensuring safety, reliability and economical operation in order to reduce any space tourism traveler personal worry to catch any spacecraft.

So, the space tourism safe journey plan is one very important factor to influence space tourism consumer number for them if any one of space tourism leisure business hoped they can grow the space tourism consumer number for long term. For example, the space boat flight hardware must often be maintained at the space station. It is needed to be considered by space boat experts as risky, extremely expensive and potentially sensitive. To aims to ensure spacecraft will offer an economical and safe alternative for any satellite manufacturers and other space tourism entertainment organizations have a desire or requirement for space tourism flight.

(2) reduction cost expense plan

On second aspect concerns reduction cost expense plan, any space tourism entertainment organizations need have the experience and capacity for safely launching a fully loaded , including space tourism passengers and passenger individual cargo for every spacecraft tourism journey. As a result of outsourcing the launch role to a major contractor, the space tourism pilot can concentrate on space boat crews flight training, planning space tourism passenger cargo capacity and preparing space flight manifests , and will as a result, avoid the expense of maintaining a launch operation on a daily basis. In addition, by outsourcing the spacecraft manufacturing, it can avoid spending millions of dollar on facilities and equipment infrastructure and engineering manufacturing expertise.

(3) achieve any space tourism mission plan

On third aspect concerns how to achieve any space tourism mission. Every space tourism mission must be ensure that reliable service is provided to satisfy every space tourism passenger personal space traveler needs and let them to enjoy in their whole space tourism journey, let them to catch a big aircraft in comfortable environment of technologically sophisticated space boat, reasonable and competitive every time space tourism flight ticket price plan is developed and properly revised every time space tourism ticket price when performing their assigned every different space tourism journey mission.

Hence, the space tourism leisure company will provide one careful selected space tourism destination , e.g. Mar planet space tourism journey, Moon planet space tourism journey or no any space destination journey, it means that the space craft only needs to fly one circle around between Earth and Moon space journey etc. that are capable of meeting the requirements of travelling into Earth orbit. So, any space tourism journey must emphasize affordability, reliability, safety, customer service and responsiveness in responding to every client's space tourism journey requirements. Hence, any one of space tourism journey must have clear space journey mission and objective to satisfy any space traveler client target needs.

● Methods to raise space traveler number

Future space tourism will be one kind of new travel leisure market for any new space travel leisure companies to enter this undiscovered market in the beginning. However, how to predict future 10 to 20 years , even more space traveler number that is one important issue to any new space tourism leisure companies.

I think that space tourism leisure companies need to define what kinds of space travel leisure service to be provided to space travelling passengers, however, what age group of space passengers who will be their space travelling target client. For example, their space travel leisure must provide any flight operation that takes one or more passengers beyond the altitude of 100 km and thus into space to let space travelling passengers who have fun, exciting space travelling feeling.

Anyway, for any kind of space tourism (leisure space travel) journey, space tourism leisure company needs anyone to be bring customer satisfaction, it is a plan or predictive methods to measure how to let every space travelling passenger to feel comfortable when they are catching the spacecraft (space flying product) and they can have enjoyable and fun or exciting feeling when they have need providing any space tourism journey, services meet or surpass customer expectations.

Thus, any space tourism leisure company needs to evaluate the degree of every time space tourism journey's customer satisfaction and customer satisfaction is also always evaluated in relationship to the every time ticket price of the space tourism journey. So, the space tourism leisure company will predict the next time of what the space tourism journey of passenger number is more accurate, after it has evaluated what degree of every time space tourism journey's customer satisfaction is. It aims to gather their opinions to find which aspects that they need to revise, e.g. choosing where will be the next time space tourism journey destination, how to improve spacecraft staff's service attitude and performance to serve to their space tourism passengers when they are catching the spacecraft, to evaluate whether the spacecraft can provide comfortable and safe environment to let them to catch in order to let the next time space travelling passengers can feel satisfactory and enjoyable when they are catching the space tourism leisure's spacecraft to fly to anywhere in space.

In general, the expectation of factors space passengers include the following customer value elements, such as below:

- viewing space and the Earth.
- experiencing weightlessness and being able to float freely in zero gravity.
- experiencing pre-flight astronaut training and related sensations.
- communicating from space to significant others.
- being able to discuss the adventure in an informed way.
- having astronaut like documentation and memorabilia.

These objectives need to be combined with, sometimes conflicting constraints, such as guaranteed safe return, limited training time, reasonable comfort, and minimum medical restrictions. All these above issues which will be every space travelling passenger considerate matters before they choose the space tourism leisure company to catch its spacecraft to fly to space. So, all these factors will influence the next time space passenger number. Any space tourism leisure company can not neglect how to solve these all matters before they decide when their next time space tourism journey to be achieved.

Consequently, if the space craft tourism leisure company could revise what aspects of its last space tourism journey to find what are its wrong or weakness or unattractive challenges to cause any one space travelling passenger who feels unsatisfactory. Then, it can have more effort to concentrate on improving its next space tourism journey to raise its space tourism service performance level , e.g. people, food, leisure etc. service aspects and its space tourism product quality level, e.g. proving comfortable spacecraft facilities to let space travelling passengers to catch in whole spacecraft tourism journey. Then, it will have more confidence to achieve the raising space travelling passenger number.

● What is the prediction space travelling passenger desire method ?

The prediction space travelling passenger individual desire method can be one survey investigation method. When every time spacecraft finishes space tourism journey mission, after all space tourism passengers catch the spacecraft to arrive earth from space. When they arrive earth space station destination, then the space tourism leisure company can arrange survey investigation staffs to enquire their feeling for this time space tourism journey immediately.

The survey content can include as below:

Do you feel satisfactory or unsatisfactory to which aspects of this time space tourism journey?

(1) On service aspect questions include as below:

(a) Do you feel space food taste is good?

(b) Do you enjoy this time space tourism journey arrangement?

(c) Do you feel satisfactory to space staff
service performance?

(d) If you have unsatisfactory feeling for any one of above questions, which aspect issue cause you feel unsatisfactory to explain to let us to know in order to us to revise our service performance.

(2) On product aspect questions include as below:

(a) Do you feel comfortable when you are catching our spacecraft in whole space tourism journey?

(b) If you feel comfortable , may you explain the reasons what aspects of our spacecraft has weakness to cause you feel uncomfortable?

(c) Do you feel safe when you are catching our spacecraft in whole space tourism journey?

(d) If you feel unsafe, may you explain the reasons what aspects of our spacecraft has weakness to cause you feel unsafe?

Finally, we thank your ideas to be given to let us know how to improve our every time future space tourism journey in order to find what challenge cause our service performance and product quality which can not satisfy your needs. So, we shall improve to avoid future challenges continue occur. Our mission is achievement of 100% satisfactory level to our every space travelling passenger individual feeling. Also, we hope that you can choose our space tourism leisure service again, when you have another time space tourism leisure desire need. However, we shall revise to improve our service performance and product quality to be better, after collecting your ideas from this time survey investigation. I think you spend time to give your ideas from this survey investigation faithfully.

So, survey investigation method will be one important idea gathering tool to help any space tourism leisure company to revise the weaknesses to raise or improve future every time space tourism journey service performance and product quality to achieve raising competitive effort in this new space tourism leisure market.

Hence, survey investigation method will be the best idea gathering method to predict how space travelling passenger emotion or desire need will change in order to achieve the objective of raising every time space tourism journey future space travelling passenger number more easily for every space tourism leisure company.

- The prediction of price factor influences space traveler number

The space tourism leisure organizations indicate the total cost of a trip into space is rapidly coming down from the initial price level of about US$600,000, it is obvious that the space travelling customer base is going to be rather small. Typical customers tend to belong to the top 1% income bracket. They also indicate that the price comes down , it is expected that new space travelling customer groups will enter the space tourism leisure market.

Typical new customers include people in other brackets with one-of-a kind incomes, such as inheritance or business sold. There are indications that those types of customers are becoming interested in spending on an once-in-a lifetime space experience. Therefore, the growth of the space tourism market is highly sensitive to customer satisfaction and how it is communicated through various media.

This will establish the status factors of space tourism and corresponding brand reputation service providers. They also suggest that any operator monitors space travelling customer satisfaction closely, as it will help developing increasingly accurate estimates of how the space tourism leisure market will develop.

Hence, it seems that every time space tourism journey price variable factor will influence the time space tourism of customer individual leisure desire and the space tourism passenger number. For example, the minimum price goal foe a variable space tourism business is currently estimate to be below US$3000-4000/kg for a round -trip depending on variable configuration and operation size. At this price, they estimate that somewhat over 1 % of the high income earners are potential customers.

However, for significant volume growth the longer term goal should be below US$2000/kg for a typical passenger, baggage and supplies. The lower price will probably open space tourism to a broader population, expanding the customer base and altering expectations. beyond this point space tourism will become into a travelling competitive leisure commodity, price competition will ensure and service providers need to rethink their space tourism marketing and branding and price strategies.

I shall also recommend how to attract the potential customers successfully. First, space operators need to pay special attention to the right level of customer services. Second, various preparatory customer operations cost, such as a travel to the launch site, space tourism destination accommodation, pre-flight training, medical check-ups and equipment my add up to between 10 to 15 % of the actual space travel cost. Thurs, solving the right balance between services offered and cost of client operation in order to earn the largest intangible benefits, such as loyalty, confidence, leisure enjoyment, comfortable space travelling journey as well as tangible benefits, such as profit, spacecraft manufacturing facilities, space stations, space hotels , space swimming pools, space gardens, space cinema etc. which are built to similar to earth building facilities to satisfy space travelers‘ needs.

Nowadays, our earth is no longer an adventurous enough place for some experienced tourists. Space tourism will be a new sector of adventure tourism, which is in the near future will be fast becoming a new tourism leisure opportunity for experiencing the unknown. Of one day, space tourism is able to reach the mass tourism phase, due to improved safety and decreased operation costs, a future space tourist will possibly only need minimal training to cope with the zero cost.

Space tourism is quite well established with visits to space attraction and launch sites, and it is a wealthy trips to the international space station for any space tourism travelers. However, if any space tourism leisure companies can attempt to find what the most influential factors are to persuade travelers feel attraction more than travelling in our earth.

It aims to let travelers to choose space travelling more than earth travelling when they feel travelling leisure need. I shall indicate what will be the most important influential factors to persuade travelers to choose space tourism more than earth tourism as below:

Firstly, I shall argue that the majority of different new space tourism journey destinations will be needed to find to satisfy different aged space travelers and different income space tourism consumers' needs. For example, the rich people have effort to consume longer time and reach any space tourism destinations where are far away from our earth of their every space tourism journey.

Otherwise, the middle income people will choose shorter space tourism journey distance from our earth and short time space tourism journey. Also, younger space tourism clients can accept more longer journey time, exciting fast speed spacecraft flying journey. Otherwise, old space tourism clients can only accept comfortable and shorter time safe space journey. So, it seems that safety, comfortable feeling, shorter time space tourism journey won't be one important influential factor to excite any young people who choose to consume space tourism leisure. Otherwise, safety, comfortable feeling, shorter time space tourism journey will be one important influential factor to excite any old people who choose to consume space tourism leisure.

Secondly, the another most important influential factor to excite space travelers to choose space tourism , it concerns whether the space travelers will feel what tourists benefits can be earned from a substantial variety of destinations choice. In general, space tourism with those of aviation, space travelers will hope space tourism will be travelling distances by air in a very short time, safely and comfortably, to bring them to arrive any space planet destinations when spacecraft reaches any space stations to stay in any space destinations.

Hence, space destination factor will bring important influential choice to any space destination journeys. As a result of the space technological tourism boom, the number of potential different space destination, choice attractions have grown with far fewer places on earth to which human do have access yet. However, the ultimate different space destinations to which many of us dream is not on earth, but as least 100 km above us, anywhere in space any planets.

If the space tourism leisure company can provide different space tourism destination choices to young or old age both space traveler target consumer groups. They will feel a real holiday when they will be able to enjoy a great image of the earth from planets. It might mean that every space tourism journey can provide different space tourism destination to let space travelers have another new travelling destinations where are far from our earth anywhere.

Hence, the different space tourism destinations will give them an unforgettable adventure. Think of how it would be to be able to check in at a " billion strategy" luxury hotel in space one planet, it means that the space planet destination can provide one luxury hotel to let space travelers to live one night or more in the space planet destination, how it would be to schedule the space traveler' vacation at one of the space tourism leisure company luxury resorts on the Moon or Mars.

This images seem from science fiction movies, but one should not forget that 100 years ago, the Wright brothers, aviation pioneers inventors and builders of the air plane, would not have imagined how, every day it is possible that future spacecraft can fly to any planets to let human have chance to stay in the space hotel one night or more.

Consequently, space destination choice and space tourism journey service performance, aviation safety, ticket price and leisure satisfactory feeling which will be important influential factors to attract future space travelers to choose space tourism leisure to replace earth tourism leisure in future one day.

● Raising space tourism leisure
consumption strategies

Although, space tourism industry is a real enjoyment and exciting travelling leisure to human. It is possible that human will choose to consume space tourism leisure to replace earth tourism leisure, if human felt that earth tourism leisure is not attractive to them to consume to go to anywhere to travel in their leisure time.

But, I believe that space tourism industry has still many factors to influence human to choose to consume space tourism leisure, even they will consider space tourism leisure consumption I is only one time space tourism in their life time. Hence, space tourism companies ought achieve this aim to persuade or attract everyone prefer to spend space tourism leisure at least one time in their life, then it can represent success. However, I think to achieve this aim, it has these challenges to influence their success, even they believe space tourism leisure business is one potential attractive travel entertainment business. These challenges include such as: expensive space tourism ticket price issue, catching spacecraft safe issue, space traveler personal body health issue, age issue, family and friend relationship influence issue, working time and holiday time arrangement issue, the space trip arrangement issue, weather issue etc. different challenges, which will have possible to influence every space tourism planner either who decide change to cancel the time space tourism plan, or forgive to choose space tourism leisure in their life forever.

Hence, how to raise space tourism leisure consumption desire will be one considerable matter for any space tourism leisure businessmen. I shall indicate my personal three aspect of strategical opinions to let them to know how to raise every space tourism planner individual space tourism leisure consumption desire to avoid every time space tourism passenger number will have decrease failure chance as below:

● (1) Strategic opinion

On the first aspect of strategic opinion, I feel that the space education tutor can teach new space knowledge to let every space traveler to learn any new space and earth knowledge during he/she is catching on the spacecraft in personal contact learning experience environment which can raise space tourism consumption desire. The reason is because the space tourism leisure traveler can raise extra space and earth learning knowledge when they can catch the spacecraft to fly and contact the space environment to learn and feel what the differences are between space and earth by himself or herself. Hence, it is very attractive to the space traveler student target group and I believe that their parents will encourage their sons or daughters to participate the time of space trip and they are more preferable to help them to buy the time space trip ticket, due to their sons and daughters can learn any space knowledge when they are studying. Moreover, every space traveler will feel surprise to learn any new space and earth knowledge from the space tutor's teaching, due to he/she is unknown that this space travel trip includes learning space and earth knowledge.

I suggest that the space tourism leisure businessmen can give learning opportunity to every travel trip space travelers to feel that this space actual environment can bring what disadvantages or advantages to influence our earth when they are catching aircraft to fly to space to travel in every space

trip. The space and earth learning knowledge can include these two aspects of space learning knowledge and experience below:
On the teaching of space environment learning knowledge hand, the topics can include as below:
Firstly the space learning topic can concern how space environment influences water and hydrated minerals change , they can learn what our drinking water function how is applied to space environment. For example, in the space environment, they can learn and attempt to feel that how water can be used in protecting astronauts against harmful radiation from the sun and cosmic rays by cloaking spacecraft with a thin layer of water in the actual space environment as well as the space travelers can also feel water is same as fuel when they are catching the spacecraft, they can feel the water is heavy to transport into space when they are catching the spacecraft to fly to space during their whole space tourism journey.
Moreover, when their spacecraft reaches anyone of planets and it stays on the planet's space station, e.g. Moon space station. They can learn how to attempt to contact the hydrated minerals to learn and feel what they contained in some asteroids may be possible sources of water and fuel in the actual space environment. When they are walking in actual space environment, such as Moon planet, they can contact or touch this hydrated minerals to learn how water molecules can be extracted and separated chemically to produce hydrogen fuel knowledge in the actual space environment. This is one exciting space learning experience to the space travelling student passengers.
Secondly the space learning topic can concern how human fights space threats , even when their whole space leisure journey, the space science teacher can let the space trip student passengers to feel that they are learning new space knowledge between the space science teacher and whose space trip student passengers. Such as how to protect our earth knowledge: Teaching them to know when will be threats to our earth from space. The space science teacher can explain how this space threating environment influences our life safety and let them to feel that a mass extinction can be triggered if an asteroid 10 kilometers across hit the earth. Even being the apex species in the food chain did not space carnivorous dinosaurs from such disaster, who knows if this terrifying scene won't happen before our eyes? So, the space travelers can image and feel how the space threating environment can influence their life safety in the actual space environment as well as the space science teacher can let whose space

travelers to feel and image the actual earth disaster will possible happen suddenly to let they feel afraid in the actual space environment. Also the space science teacher can teach how our earth can fright the space stones attack to let the space traveler to know, when an impactor targets an asteroid for a controlled well-times wallop. The collision will change the asteroid's momentum, deflecting it from its original orbital path which intersects with that of the earth. So, at the moment, the space travelers can image they are a larger spacecraft near an asteroid which can also change the path. Given enough time, the gravitational pull from the spacecraft will be able to steer the asteroid away from the earth. So, every space traveler will feel that they are catching the spacecraft in the safe space environment to avoid the Earth disaster from space sudden unpredictable attack.

It is more fun real space tourism knowledge learning feel to let every space traveler has chance to learn any new space science knowledge when he/she is catching the spacecraft to fly to space to travel. Hence, one successful space trip ought include trip and learning experience both contents in order to raise every the space tourism planner individual space trip consumption desire.

● (2) Strategic opinion

On the second aspect of strategic opinion, space tourism leisure companies need to let planning travelers feel that anyone of space tourism leisure is very different to general tourism leisure. In general, tourism leisure is visiting at least one night for leisure and holiday, business or other tourism purposes in Earth only. Otherwise, space tourism leisure is other kind of an unique trip leisure or entertainment method, e.g. the space traveler can catch the spacecraft to visit any planets to stay to live at the planet's space hotel at least one night, e.g. Future potential populated Moon or Mars space hotel space trip. Moreover, the space travel companies ought give chance to let them to feel what weightless feeling is in weightlessness environment when they are walking on Moon or other planets in possible. Even, they can attempt to build these entertainment facilities, instead of space hotels, such as space swimming pools, space gardens, space cinema etc. building facilities. It aims to let them to feel what the differences between Earth and space life when they are walking on the Moon, when they are swimming on the space pools, when they are living in space hotels, when they are watching movies in space cinemas, when they are seeing flowers and different species of planets and fruits. e.g. oranges, apples, bananas, and vegetable and potatoes and tomatoes in space gardens. It is very exciting and fun space trip life experience between one days to seven days. So, they believe that they must not feel these space life experience if they do not choose to participate this time space trip planning journey by the space trip company preparation.

Also, due to that the space tourism passengers need to the pre-flight checks and training before they ensure to qualify to permit to participate the space trip. So space travel companies need to concern how to take care their health check and training matter considerately. It aims to let every space traveler will feel a market segment with fitness and extreme experiences as well as he/she will become popular with a market segment passenger to the space tourism leisure company, although he/she must not guarantee to pass the space training and/or pre-flight health checks to permit to participate the space trip. However, he/she can believe that he/she is one worth space travelling passenger to the space tourism leisure company, even this time pre-flight health check or/and the short time space trip training requirements are failure. However, the space tourism leisure company must need to let all pre-flight health check and space trip training passengers to feel that it is only one space tourism which can give them and let customers view the space travel is as the ultimate showcase for health, even though a majority of the population can pass the pre-flight medical and other tests in order to raise their confidence and safety to catch the spacecraft to fly to space to travel when they are confirmed to pass these tests to permit to catch the spacecraft later.

In general, the expectations of future space passengers include the following customer value elements, such as below:

- Viewing space and the Earth.
- Experiencing weightlessness and experiencing pre-flight astronaut training and related sensations.
- Communicating from space to significant others.
- Being able to discuss the adventure in an informed way.
- Having astronaut-like documentation and memorabilia.
- Enjoying one exciting and fun space trip.

However, instead of considering these objectives need to be combined with, sometimes conflicting , constraints such as guaranteed safe, return , limited training time, reasonable comfort, and minimum medical restrictions. So, space tourism companies need to reduce every space traveler individual worries before they decide to make the time of space tourism journey. Then, it can increase their confidence to raise their space tourism consumption desire more successfully.

Consequently, instead of these consideration, a space travel operator must pay attention to the total customer experience over the entire customer process, starting from how the service is presented, proposed and sold. The service package must include training, instructions, travel to the launch site and various post. Travel activities to generate maximum customer satisfaction and brand building opportunity.

(3) Strategic opinion

On the final aspect of strategic opinion, I think any space tourism companies space tourism companies need to consider every time space tourism ticket price and space tourism trip issues. It is important factor to influence every space traveler individual consumption desire. Due to space trip ticket price must be more expensive to compare common Earth trip travelling ticket price, so this kind of tourism leisure market target customer will be the rich and high income customer group.

On the space trip ticket challenge issue, despite that fact the total cost of a trip into space is rapidly coming down from the initial price level of about US$60,000, it is obvious that the customer base is going to be rather small and the client target customer is only high income or rich consumer group. Typical customers tend to belong to the top of the top 1% income bracket. So, ensures that space traveler number must be less than common Earth traveler number.

Also, such as the space trip ticket price, it is expected that new middle rich level or middle high level income customer target group will enter the space trip leisure market, when every space trip ticket price falls down about 1% Typical new customers include people in other income brackets with one-of-a-kind incomes, such as inheritance or business sold space traveler target group. These people will be space travel new client group, when its every space trip ticket price can be reduced to close 1 to 2 % nearly. If any space tourism leisure companies expect to attract new rich and/or high income target customer group to choose any one kind of space trip journey planning to consume.

These are indications that these types of customers are becoming interested in spending on an once-in-a-lifetime space experience. Therefore, the growth of the space tourism market is highly sensitive to customer satisfaction and how it is communicated through the various media. This will establish the status –factor of space tourism, and corresponding brand reputation of service providers. The minimum price goal for a variable space tourism business is currently estimate to be below US$3-4000/kg for a round-trip depending on vehicle configuration. So, space travel leisure companies need to concern every round space trip cost, it can depend on the space vehicle number and weight issue to influence every space trip ticket price variable to achieve how much it can earn.

On space journey design factor aspect, it includes these different facilities aspects how to design, because future space travelling consumers will concern whether the space travel company can provide special entertainment to satisfy their needs. The facilities include as below:

How to design space hotels to let them to live in comfortable space environment and eat the best taste and fresh food quality when the cookers need to cook in the space hotel in the space environment? How to design space swimming pools to let them to swim in safe space environment? How to design space sport centers to let them to run more easily in one space sport warm and safe environment? How to design one space garden to let them to see different species of Earth flowers, or plants? How to design one space farming land to let them to see different species of Earth fruits, vegetables, tomatoes, potatoes etc. fresh foods growth in warm and safe space farming land environment? How to design one space cinema to let them to watch movies in one safe and warm space cinema environment? All these facilities will be any one of future space trip's' important and attractive space trip leisure facilities to influence every space traveler to choose to buy the space tourism leisure company's space trip leisure service.

Instead of these space building entertainment facilities, they also need to concern how the space vehicle entertainment tools are provided the entertainment service to satisfy their needs. When the space travelers can sit on the space vehicles to move on any planets' lands, such as Moon. A number of space vehicle options exist in the market, mainly differing based on the seat capacity as well as the in-flight experience level offered. The typical space vehicle solution is a small, relatively light weight spacecraft taking between 2 to 10 passengers. The number of passengers depends on the service level, amenities and extra offered. The trip typically lasts about 10 hours and of which about 4 hours are spent in space. The main attraction is the weightless time after in space. The main attraction is the weightless time after re-entry has started. It is a rather low-G technology and therefore the medical requirements for participants are nor very high.

Consequently, the space vehicles, space leisure building facilities, the space trip reasonable price ticket level, every safe space trip journey arrangement, clean and fresh and good taste space food arrangement, space traveler individual real learning experience etc. these factors will be the main influential factors to raise the space tourism leisure company's competitive effort and the space traveler consumer individual consumption desire to the space tourism leisure company in the future.

Research how to raise space traveler individual leisure desire

The first factor may raise space traveler leisure desire is that space rocket needs have safe and clean inside environment. Future, space tourism may be another kind of possible popular tourism leisure activity, because since COVID 19 disease occurs, it may influence many travellers feel afraid to catch air planes in the high risk closed window airt plane inside environment, when many different countries people must need to body contact or air contact. Hence, it is possible that our tourism leisure will not be popular in our earth, if COVID 19 disease , even other unknown air disease may occur to cause global travellers feel fear to catch air planes to avoid life danger in the one hour, even more than 12 hours sitting air plane flying time. Otherwise, because any space tourism rockets are small and it only allows one to four space travellers and space rocket pilot to sit in the space rockets as well as any space journey is only spent 15 minutes to 30 minutes for view moon space journey or more than one day visiting moon space journey or up to one week visiting space station journey in the space rockets. So, owning COVID 19 disease travellers can permit to sit in the space rocket, the chance is low to get COVID 19 disease when the space rocket has less passengers are sitting in the space rocket. It means that when many space travellers feel any space rocket is safe and clean in the inside none window space rocket environment, this safe and clean space rocket inside environment feeling, it cam emcourage many future space passengers begin to choose to catch any one space rocket to leave earth to fly to space to travel in possible. Hence, when space rocket can be invented to bring equipment safe and comfortable feeling and guarantees none of any one owning COVID 19 disease patient can sit in the space rocket as well as all of they can catch this space rocket to earth and come back to earh safely . It means that any one space tourism leisure service provider can guarantee without any sudden accidents occurrence in space. The another most important factor may be every space tourism can charge reasonable ticket price to any one space trip to let any one space tourism leisure consumer to feel. All of these factors may influence the space tourism leisure consumers number increases to the space tourism leisure service provider.

Instead of above space trip ticket price and space rocket's safe and clean inside environment both aspects. I shall indicate how to raise space traveller individual leisure desire methods as below:

Firstly. attractive space trip is another important factor to influence any one space tourism leisure consumers to choose the space tourism leisure service provider's any one space tourism leisure activities. Because of the space trip's time is short, e.g. 15 minutes to 30 minutes leaving earth to stay on space for viewing our earth leisure , within this 15 to 30 minutes short space trip time, the space tourism leisure service provider needs to seek the different kinds of attractive space destinations to let every space tourism leisure passengers to feel enjoyable in space different locations when they see our earth from their rocket's staying different locations in space. Because different space locations, they can influence different viewing feeling of our earth from the rocket. So, choosing the suitable different space locations to stay in order to view earth , this short time space staying locations trip is very important to influence every passenger whose viewing earth feeling. Otherwise, if the space trip's time is longer, e.g. more than 5 hours sitting to visit moon space trip. The space trip must need to be arrangement have more attractive feeling to let they do not feel boring when they need to sit more than 5 hours in the space rocket to arrive the moon. So, their sitting space rocket times are needed to be feel leisure times for every passenger. They can not feel bore or non space trip arrangement leisure feeliing in the whole space trip. So, when the space trip is longer time, its space leisure activities arrangement ought need have enough different leisure activities to provide in order to avoid any one space passenger feels bore, e.g. spending one week to arrive space station space trip, the rocket must need have sport equipment or cinema provide to let they do not feel bore when they need to sit about one week time to go to the space station as well as spend another one week time to come back earth from the space station. Otherwise, short time space trip , e.g. only 15 minutes viewing earth space trip , it doe not any space trip leisure activities, because this space viewing earth trip aims to let passengers can feel comfortable and enjoyable to view our earth when they are sitting in the rocket in this 15 minutes. However, this rocket needs to fly to about 4 to 5 different space locations to let passengers to feel different viewing earth visable feeling. If the rocket is only staying in one same space location to let them to view our earth. They must feel bore to view the same visable feeling of our earth in this 15 minutes space viewing earh trip. So, space locations choice factor is very important for short time viewing earth space trip. Consequently, they may feel their this short time viewing earth space trip ticket price is unreasonable.

Hence, any one space trip lesiure activities and space staying locations choice arrangement, as well as its space trip time as well as its evaluated ticket price, they must have close relationship to influence any one space trip traveller individual leisure satisfactory feeling in this space tourism leisure development industry. Hence, if any one space tourism leisure service provider hopes that they can have many space travellers to choose their any one long or short time space trip lesisure activities. They must need to consider how to design space trip in order to attract their leisure choices , how to evaluate every space trip's time and space trip ticket price in order to achieve how to attract many future space traveller individual preference space trip choice among potentient different space trip lesiure providers. Because when future space tourism leisure is popular to accept. In this space tourism market, it will have many potential space tourism leisure service providers attempt to anticipate and implement any kinds of space trip leisure activities arrangement, it seems future space trip may influence our traditional tourism industry from earth travel changes to space travel lesisure direction development.

In earth tourism industry, every travel leisure service provider needs to design different kinds of travelling destinations in order to attract different countries travellers choose to play themselves designing trips packages, if their trips arrangements are attrractive, it will influence thr traveller chooses this travel agent's trip to visit the another country service. Hence, earth trip's travelling packages are very important to influence every traveller individual travel agent choice. It seems that space tourism trip arrangement may be another main factor to influence space passengers number increases or decreases to any one space leisure service provider. The question concerns how to design attract space trip to any one space traveller choice preference. I shall explain as below:

IN fact, space tourism's general price is expensive, so the wealthiest people ought be any ones space tourism leisure provider's main customer target. But advances in rocket and capsule design also also expected to lower the price to the point that people of more modest fortunes are able to afford a ticket. What space tourists can expect? What exactly is on store for space tourists? The excitment of a rocket ride and a chance to experience weightlessness for starters. And bragging rights are hard to beat. But some the biggest benefit of point into space is getting a dramatic new outlook on life when any one space traveller can try to catch rocket to leave our earth home.

For Virgin Galactic plans to offer suborbital space trips, with customers being treated to feel of weightlessness feeling. He says more than 600 customers have signed contracts to already to pay a ticket price US$250,000 for one time space trip. Another space tourism leisure provider, e.g. Blue Origin, Amazon CEO Jeff Bezos , thees space tourism leisure providers had begun to plan future space adventures leisures to satisfy future any one space traveller individual space trip leisure need. In general, average a ticket price is between US$75,000 to US$300,000. SO, wealth people must be space travel consumer targert customer.

Future space trip may include: Flying to space stations, it may be a big vacation will be able to buy a rocket ride into orbit, future NASA is not transfoming into a space travel agency, private companies will have to pay it about US$35,000 a night per passenger to sleep in the space station's beds and use its amenities, including air, water , the internet and toilet. Hence, flying to space station may be one attract one to two weeks attractive space trip.

Another kind of space trips, such as a variety of options for private of spaceflight have started to emergy. Virgin Galactic, founded by the entrepreneur Richard Branson, and Blue Origin from Jeffrey P. Benos of Amazon, both plan to carry passengers on short suborbital flights, space X also announced that Yusaka Maezawa, a Japanese, clothing company founder, would pay for a trip around the moon on a spacecraft it is building. Hence, short time space trip, e.g. flying to moon or leaving earth short suborbital flights, staying on space to viewing our earth , even long time space trip, e.g. flying to space station,spends more than one to two weeks. They may be future any one wealth space traveller's space trip leisure choice.

Some companies already conduct modest experiments on the space station, such as Merall Research laboratories, which has grown crystals of antibodies, and mode in space, which is testing the manufacture of higher quality optical communications fiber in the weightlessness of orbit. Hence, flying to moon and staying on space to viewing our earth space trips both ticket prices miust be more cheaper to compare long time spce trip, e.g. visiting space stations space trip. Axion space, a houston based company that arranges training and all aspects of the flights, is charging as much as US$55 million for a week long trip to the international space station. Blus Origin , Virgin Galactic had been planning attractive space trip. It focuses on views of earth space leisure activities when its space travelling customers can sit in its space rocket. Virgin Galactic was charging as much as US$250, 000 per seat on its spaceship. HOwever, these both space planes have a waiting list of about 600 passengers.

ON conclusion, in the future, the different kinds of space trips may include: short journey viewing earth, 15 to 30 minutes, visiting to moon, about one days , even it is possible that visiting space station, one to two weeks. Even it is possible that any one space traveller can attempt to live one night in space hotel, if human can build hotels on moon, when human can confirm moon can build hotels , then flying to moon to live one night space trip experience may be implement in possible. I believe that any one space leisure provider can attract many space passengers to choose their viewing earth short time staying space trip, visiting moon, living space hotels, visiting space stations to live one night space leisure trip, So, any one space trip leisure provider can attempt to evaluaate whether implementing "living moon hotel" or " visiting space station" or viewing our earth any one space trip is possible in order to raise future any one potential space traveller individual leisure desire. However, the main considerable points, they need to evaluate whether they ought charge how much space trip ticket or seat price for every passenger. Also, they need build confidence to let every passenger feels their space rocket is safe to sit to leave our earth and come back our earth again absolutely. Hence, all of these are important factors to influence future any one space tourism leisure provider their success, if they expect to develop their space trips businesses in long time.

Development space tourism successful factors

Space tourism passengers leisure feeling

In future tourism leisure development, if we hope to develop our future space tourism entertainment in success, we need to know how to persuade general rich people how to make decision to choose to catch which kinds of rockets to travel outer space, because many of they will feel space is horror when they need to stay at the strange dark low degree temperature and none heavy weight body body feeling environment space environment. When they catch the rocket to visit the dark space strange environment.

In common, any space rocket passengers may usually feel dangerous , when their space rocket is crashed by any space stones suddenly. If one big size space stone flys toward to the space rocket direction to crash suddenly, due to the space rocket can not predict when any space stones will fly toward to this space rocket to crash it suddenly. Hence, space strange dark environment may influence many space tourism passengers feel fear to catch space rocket to fly in space environment in long time.

However, although flying to space environment toursim which may bring exciting and pleasure and enjoyment feeling to any one when they are catching the space rocket to fly to future space station, moon, even fly to space hotel to live one night or more, or stay the rocket to view our earth in different space environment locations for several minutes etc. different kinds of space tourism journeys. But, when the space rocket stays longer time in space environment, then it may bring more dangerous to the space rocket and the space passenger individual life both. Because many different kinds of space accidents may occur, e.g. space rocket has fire happens, machine equipment is damaged, space stones crash the rocket, space steel rubblishs crash the roctket, even space rocket windows may be damaged by any things etc. So, different kinds of accidents may be difficult to predict. Also, it implies that we may ensure any kinds of space rockets have chance to occur accidents when they are staying in the strange and dark space environment in any time.

Consequently, it will bring fear feeling to let any one space tourism passenger feel afraid to catch the space rocket to travel space long time. In special, if the space tourist is very rich, he must feel his life is value, he ought not lose his life due to this space rocket is crashed by any space stones, or space rubblishd ot itself damage factor etc. different space accidents occurrence. Hence, if any one space tourism service provider hopes that it can encourage many space tourists choose to catch itself space rocket in preference. It must need to let many its space rocket passengers feel itself space rocket is more safer or brings more safe feeling to let its all space rocket passengers to feel. Moreover, its needs to let many space tourism passengers may feel its space rocket is more safe to compare other space tourism leisure service providers their space rockets facilities.

Consequently, there are many space tourists may be influenced to choose to catch this space tourism lesiure service provider's space rocket to fly to space, because if they feel other space tourism leisure service providers , their space rockets are not safe to compare this space tourism leisure service provider's space rocket. Then, this space tourism leisure service provider may design different kinds of unique space journeys in order to let any space tourist feel more safe to stay longer time in space environment. Hence, it may help any one space leisure tourism service provider raise to charge higher ticket fee when its every space journey is longer time to compare general short time space journeys.

Is right time to develop space tourism lesiure

Nowadays, human can have different kinds of lesiure choices. They may include tourism in ourselves earth, sports, visiting cinemas to see movies, listening musics, reading ebooks or paper books, visitng theatre to see art performances, seeing paints etc. any every different kinds of lesiure activities. However, comparing among of any kinds of general lesisures, tourism lesiure must be the most expensive kind of entertainment activity to compare all of above these different kinds of lesiure activities. Hence, it brings this question: Is right time to develop space tourism leisure market?

In fact, future human travel choice has only these both kinds: One is travelling in ourselves earth, another is catching rocket to travel space, e.g. visiting space station, staying on space one location to view ourselves earth or moon, or visiting moon, living space hotel one night or more etc. different kinds of space tourism leisure activities. However, I beleive that it is right time to develop space tourism leisure. I shall explain as below:

The first reason, all of us ought know that this kind of disease COVID 19 had influenced global many travellers had began to feel fear to catch air planes to go to other countries to travel because many travellers began to believe that they may get this kind of illness easily when any one of air plane passengetr is sitting close to the COVID 19 patient, even any one air plane passenger may also be gotten by air when any one COVID 19 patient is sitting in the close window air plane seat. Hence, COVID 19 disease is significant to influence global many travellers began to reduce to catch any air planes to go to any countries to travel frequently, even the having travelling habit travellers will choose not travelling any countries any times by air planes.

So, it seems that COVID 19 disease will have long time to influence futuer global tourism leisure market development in our earth. It is one negative psychological factor of " feeling afraid to catch air plane" to any one liking tourism leisure tourist. So, when one likes often to go to other countries to travel, in special, the high income or rich people group, when they feel fear to need to catch air planes to go to other countries to travel, they must feel bore, due to they must only stay in themselves home countries by COVID

19 disease attacks. In fact, although these high income or rich people tourist group can choose any kinds of leisures to replace tourism leisure activity, e.g. sport, going to cinemas to see movies, going to concert halls to listen musics or songs, going to theatres to see art performances. But, all of these different kinds of entertainment activities can not satisfy themselves leisure psychological needs, because they have much money, they like to spend money to go to any countries to travel for one week, or two weeks , even one month more in their holidays.

Nowadays, because this kind of COVID 19 disease influences they feel afraid to catch air planes to travel to any countries frequently. They avoid to catch air planes to contact any one, he/she may have COVID 19 diease, even when they arrive the traveling destination, they none COVID 19 disease travellers , they feel that their bodies may be goten COVID 19 disease, when they need visit any one hotel to rent rooms to live, or rent appartments to live, they must need to live strange hotel room. However, the hotel room may be lived by any one COVID 19 patient, when the tourist choose to live the hotel room, he will have chance to get COVID 19 disease due to he contact any things in the hotel room. Even, any one tourist needs to catch any train, bus, tram, taxi, ferry , underground train etc. different kinds of public transport tools, they may have chance to get COVID 19 disease when they are catching the public transport tool, if it has any one COVID 19 disease passenger is catching the same bus or other kinds of public transport tool, or they need to go to any one restaurants to eat breakfasts, lunchs, or dinners, they need to sit the table with the COVID 19 patient together, ot they need to walk on the streets or they need to climb mountains or they need to visit any travelling destinations etc. to do any kinds of travelling leisure activities, that they need to do in their travelling jounrneys. So, it implies that they have chance to bring COVID 19 disease to themselves bodies due to they have chance to contact any one strange person in any travelling destinations. Hence, they will feel that they may be contacted to get COVID 19 disease , when they are staying in the travelling country.

Consequently, it seems that COVID 19 siease may be one important factor to influenc global any one feels afraid to catch air planes to go to anywhere to travel. SO, such as the special rich travellers group, they only have another travel choice to replace tourism in earth, it is " visiting space tourism". Although , every tecket for any one kind of space tourism , it may be very expensive, but for this special rich traveller groups, their space

tourism leisure needs ought not be influenced reduce by expensive ticket factor easily. Because they feel that space tourism will be only another kind of expensive lesiure activity to replace tourism leisure in our earth.
The another reason is that global rich people number had been increasing every year significant. For China and US and UK and India etc. these high population countries, their rich people number had been climbed countinue every year . Hence, it implies that future many people have effort to epend at least one time of space tourism leisure, due to rich people number had been increasing in countinue. Moreover, many habit travellers began to feel that our earth has none any value destinations to visit, when they had visited any one travelling destinations at least one time. So, when many travellers feel that they had attempted to visit any vaue travelling destinations, then they won't like to buy air ticket to visit any one of these travelling destinations again. So, the only one tourism choice, is that visiting to space 's any destinations, e.g. visiting moon, visiting space stations to live one night hotel hotel, staying on space one location to vire ourselves earth or moon etc. different kinds of space journeys. Because may of rich travellers had felt that travelling in oursleves is low valur leisure and it can not attract any one rich tourist chooses this kind of lesiure again, as well as they had felr that earth has none any destinations can attract them to travel, so it is only space tourism may replace tourism in ourselves earth.
On conclusion, it is right time to prepare to invest another new kind of tourism leisure, such as space tourism , it may repalce traditional tourism in earth leisure. SO developing space tourism leisure is one value leisure developing market.

CHAPTER SIX

How robots reduce global jobs number

Can robotic invention bring social economic growth? If it is possible that why and how robotic invention can assist any countries social economic growth? But, when robots can bring economic growth, it can also influence global jobs number reduces when businesses choose to apply robots to replace human jobs, then employees number will be influenced to reduce. First, we need to know whether what economic growth means in order to answer this question. In macro economic view, economic growth may mean that GDP growth, employment ratio growth, job creating growth, unemployment ratio reduces, consumption growth, productive industries growth, service provision and service needs increases. So, it seems that any countries‘ social development , when it can have positive impact growth for any one of these issue. It implies that the country's economic is growing.

To discuss AI and economic growth issue, it may being these two main questions. Whether robotic invention may have direct or indirect relationship to influence any countries' economic growth? What are the main factors to cause robotics invention to bring the country's economic growth in its society?

On the first hand, some researchers believe that robotic invention may influence any countries‘ economic growth. However, otherwise, other many researchers find large and robust negative effects robots on employment and wages. They estimate what are more robot per thousand workers reduces the employment -to-population rate by between 0.18 and 0.34 percentage points, and is associated with a wage decline of between 0.25 and 0.5 percentage. Because many jobs can be replaced by robotics. So, it seems that robotics invention can reduce workers number and increasing wage level, even robotic increasing number, it can influence unemployment ratio increases to the country. But, some lecturers estimate that it can impact economic growth. They estimate that AI may deliver an additional economic output of around US$13 trillion by 2030 year, increasing global GDP by about 1.2% annually. This will mainly come from substitution of labour by automation and increased innovation in products and services.

What is the impact of robots on society? They may include this spillover, one robot per thousand workers has slightly less of an impact on the population as a whole, leading to an overall 0.2% point reduction in the employment-to-population ratio, and reducing wages by 0.42%. Thus, adding one robot reduces employment nationwide by 3.3 workers. So, it seems that robotic number increases may influence global workers number increases many influence global workers number reduces as the same time. It can cause unemployment workers number increases in societies.

On the other side, robotic invention can increase productivity, because robots increase productivity, which means that fewer human hours are needed to produce a given output. But, higher productivity also reduces production costs and output prices. Consequently, robotic production anticipation , it can increase the quality demanded by consumers, and firms hire workers in this increased demand.

But, when robotic production participation to any industrial manufacture, it can also bring negating effects, when they are entering the workforce, e.g. higher maintenance and installation costs to factories, enhanced risk of data breach and other cybersecurity issues, reduced flexibility, anxiety and insecurity regarding the future social development. So, it seems that robotic invention can bring the future of workplace automation may reduce workers number of factories, loss of jobs and reduced employment opportunities to global future workers, potential job lose, initial investment costs to employers. However, AI may also bring harmful to our future societies because if AI surpasses humanity in general intelligence and becomes " superintelligent" , then it could become difficult or impossible for humans to control. Moreover, a second source concern is that a sudden and unexpected " intelligence explosion" might take an unprepared human race by surprise. Hence, robotic invention may become human enemy or soldier, if human applies it to social damage aspect.

However, robotic invention can also bring advantages to our future societies in possible, robotic automation may bring advantages to employers : cost effectiveness, improved quality assurance, increased productivity, avoiding workers need to work in hazardous environments. But,. AI can also bring positive impact our daily lives, such as artificial intelligence can dramatically improve the efficiencies of our workplace and can argument the work humans can do. When AI takes over repetitive or dangerous tasks, it frees up the human workforce to do work, they are better equipped for, tasks that involve creativity and empathy among others.

However, robotic invention may bring organizational benefits in our societies. Robots will have a profound effect on the workplace of the future. They will become capable of taking on multiple roles in organizations, e.g bookkeeping or writing law draft simple clerical tasks. So, it's time for us to start thinking about the way we shall interact with our new coworkers. To be more precise, robots are expected to take over half of all low-skilled jobs in our societies, e.g. cleaning , warehouse picking up delivering tasks, restaurant cooking, hotel front line customer service, hotel room food delivery tasks etc.

So, when robots would be used in many fields all over the world. However, robots can not totally rule over the workplace by replacing all humans at jobs to keep economy afloat. Hence, robots in the workplace may bring advantages, they will not have bad emotion problems, such as safety of utilizing robotics to work in dangerous workplace. Robots do not get distracted or need to take breaks robots never need to sleep or they need to divide their attention between a multitude of things, perfection, let employees to feel happier and safe to work when robotics can help workers to work in dangerous warehouses or factories, workers can be replaced from robotics, increases productivities and job creation , even raises efficiencies in any workplaces.

In our future, whether robots won't destroy humans. It depends on how humans choose to apply this technological worker tool. A robot may not injure a human being or, though inaction, allow a human bring to come to harm. A robot must obey the orders given it by human beings, expect where such orders would conflict with the first law. A robot must protect its existence as long as such protection does not conflict with the first or second laws. How AI technology affects us in the future. They are concerned that we will see increases in stress, anxiety, and depression as digital lives expand. Meanwhile , we shall need to adapt our future digital living, there will be less face-to-face interaction , increased inactivity, poor in-person communication skills and an overall distrust among people. For robotic invention case example, future robotics can may focus on developing these five major field: Human -robotic interface, mobility, manipulation, programming, sensors and their importance to robotics development.

Robots can be applied to educational aspect. Robots can be used to bring students into the classroom that otherwise might not be able to attend. Robots such as the one mentioned are able to bring school to student who can not present physically. Simulators-high school sees the strongest example of stimulators within drivers' education courses, e.g. Google's worker robots. Google is planning to produce worker robots with personalities. So, robots can help teachers automate key classroom processes, integrate advanced technologies, acclimate students to technological change and helping identify personalized learning potential and discovering key learning trends.

● How manufacturers to raise efficiency in order to improve economic growth in possible to apply manufacturing robots to improve help economic growth

(AI) can be defined as the capability of a machine to imitate intelligent human behavior. If AI can imitate any talent humans to learn how to improve their behaviors, e.g. manufacturing industry worker behavior improves to raise GDP growth or productive number grows rapidly . Can artificial intelligence being labour to become automated? Allows an ever-in-to increasing number of tasks previously performed by human labour to become automated in the ordinary production of goods and services process.

Can (AI) create new ideas and technologies to help businessmen to solve complex problems and improve automation in the production of goods and services. The question concerns how (AI) manufacturing technology can impact economic growth?

(AI)'s new form of automation live, self-driving cars, or they may bring high levels of skill,such as legal services, radiology, and some forms of scientific lab-based research. Can it allow our societies be impacted on economic growth, due to automation to disicipline our modeling of AI.

In fact, AI automation to production of new ideas to future any industrial manufacturing process. It can influence to market structure, organization restructure, reallocation and wage inequality. So, discovering to AI automation can help future any organizations need to change existing task or discovering new tasks that can be used in production a reflects the fraction of tasks that have been automated.

It brings automating old tasks when automated could be constant, leading a stable , capital share and a stable growth rate. Hence, in long term, AI automation manufacturing technology may help businessmen to reduce large manufacturing cost in order to achieve stable micro economic benefit to them when they can apply AI automation manufacturing technologies to improve their productivities in efficient manufacturing method. For Coca Cora soft drink example, if Coca Cora applies AI automation to raise its productive soft drinks number. Then , it can manufacture many soft drinks number in short time per day. Then, its sale number can be increased, when it has enough number to supply to global to sell its soft drink. Consequently, soft drink sale number must grow rapidly significantly.

The fact that automated goods are produced with cheap capital , but it can also help business to raise production number significantly . How this superintelligence affect the economy? It seems physical tasks are essential to producing output, but when the manufacturer applies robotics to help production . Then, employees number may reduce, due to robotic participation, wages expenditure may reduce , but production number may increase .

So, AI increases the motivation at physical tasks. Hence, AI must may bring production growth innovation incentives to any manufacturers. Finally, with imitation and learning being performed mainly by super machine in developed economies. Then , research labor would become devoted to product innovations increasing product variety or inventing new products (new product lines), to replace existing products.

It is one good example to explain that how AI can bring long term social economic benefit to any manufacturers, when any old (existing) product lines are improved to innovative new product line by robotic manufacturing participation. Moreover, AI can change market structure to be reduced competition. When be escape competition effect tends to dominate at low discouragement effect may dominate for higher levels of competition or in less advanced economies. Hence , AI can also affect innovation and growth through potential effects, it might have on product market competition. So, it seems that (AI) can respond on helping social economic growth principle. On conclusion, although robotic invention may bring disadvantages to raise unemployment ratio in possible when there are many low-skilled jobs are replaced by robotics, but at the same time, robotic may be applied to education aspect, when we are experiencing digital knowledge social development stage. Hence, smart robots ought may help humans to raise economic long term growth in possible when robotics can help the developing countries to develop more rapid to be developed countries as well as they can help the developed countries to develop more advanced both in global whole one economic developed societies. So, when robots can assist any countries to cooperate together, any countries are not independent, we need robots to assist develop between countries. Then, robots can assist any countries to develop economic growth in possible in future this day comes.

How robotic helps to solve recession

Is the use of robots to job market increasing during the Great Recession? Some researchers constructed a measure of the use of robots—commonly referred to as "robot intensity"—to estimate trends in robot exposure across more than 250 metropolitan areas and over time, finding that: During the Great Recession, robot intensity plummeted. But since 2009, robot intensity has sharply increased nationwide. They felt that robots may influence recession in possible. How are robots going to affect our jobs? Most analysis tends to be prospective in nature, and estimates of future impacts on employment vary widely, with some studies predicting that as many as 50 percent of all workers are at risk of losing their jobs to automation. Even less is understood about the actual impacts of robots on jobs, wages, and workers today. If there are many low skillful jobs e.g. cleaner, warehouse deliver, cooker, restaurant waitor etc., even high skillful jobs, e.g. accountant, lawyer, doctors etc. occupations are replaced by robotics. Then, our societies will increase unemployed people number. Consequently, great recession will be caused by robotic workers because when our societies have many people lose jobs, then many people loss income, then our consumption desires may be influenced to reduce. Consequently, many businesses may lose many customers. Low consumption desires may bring serious recession to any countries, due to robotic workers number increases to replace human workers in global societies.

The reason is that new technologies of the period have enabled people to be very productive while working part-time. Businesses do not need large numbers of employees, so individuals can devote most of their waking hours to hobbies, volunteering, and community service. In conjunction with periodic work stints, they have time to pursue new skills and personal identities that are independent of their jobs. Developed countries may be on the verge of a similar transition. Robotics and machine learning have improved productivity and enhanced the economies of many nations.

Artificial intelligence (AI) has advanced into finance, transportation, defense, and energy management. The internet of things (IoT) is facilitated by high-speed networks and remote sensors to connect people and businesses. In all of this, there is a possibility of a new robotic society that could improve the lives of many people, but it also encourage future businesses apply robotics to replace human workers to do many jobs in finance, transportation, defense and energy management, medical health, hotel, tourism, cinema, theatre etc. entertainment service fields. So, robotics may bring reducing cost benefits to businessmen, but they can also increase workers losing jobs number in our societies if future many businesses make decision to apply robotics to replace human workers to do any simple ot complex jobs in global job market.

A McKinsey Global Institute analysis of 750 jobs concluded that "45% of paid activities could be automated using 'currently demonstrated technologies' and . . . 60% of occupations could have 30% or more of their processes automated."[6] A more recent McKinsey report, "Jobs Lost, Jobs Gained," found that 30 percent of "work activities" could be automated by 2030 and up to 375 million workers worldwide could be affected by emerging technologies.

Researchers at the Organization for Economic Cooperation and Development (OECD) focused on "tasks" as opposed to "jobs" and found fewer job losses. Using task-related data from 32 OECD countries, they estimated that 14 percent of jobs are highly automatable and another 32 have a significant risk of automation. Although their job loss estimates are below those of other experts, they concluded that "low qualified workers are likely to bear the brunt of the adjustment costs as the automatibility of their jobs is higher compared to highly qualified workers."

reference

James Manyika, Susan Lund, Michael Chui, Macques Bughin, Jonathan Woetzel, Parul Batra, Ryan Ko, and Saurabh Sanghui, "Jobs Lost, Jobs Gained: Workforce Transitions in a Time of Automation," McKinsey Global Institute, December, 2017.

Melanie Arntz, Terry Gregory, and Ulrich Zierahn, "The Risk of Automation for Jobs in OECD Countries," Organization for Economic Cooperation and Development, Working Paper 189, 2016.

However, some economists felt opposite opinions, they believes that future many businesses won't choose whole applying robotics to replace human workers in global job market. So, they are only human workers assistant role. Economists have, on the whole, been fairly discuss about the impact of robots and AI on workers. History is strewn with incorrect predictions of the looming irrelevance of human labour. The economic statistics have yet to signal the arrival of a robot-powered job apocalypse. Outside of slumps, firms remain keen to hire humans, for example. Growth in productivity—which ought to be surging if machines are helping fewer workers produce more output—has been unimpressive. A look beneath the aggregate numbers, though, reveals that change is indeed afoot. They believes that an AI-induced change in the mix of jobs need not translate into less hiring overall. If new technologies largely assist current workers or boost productivity by enough to spark expansion, then more AI might well go hand-in-hand with more employment. This does not appear to be happening. Instead the authors find that firms with more AI-vulnerable jobs have done much less hiring on net; that was especially the case in 2014-18, when AI-related vacancies in the database surged. But the relationship between greater use of AI and reduced hiring that is present at the firm level does not show up in aggregate data, the authors note. Machines are not yet depressing labour demand across the economy as a whole. As machines become cleverer, however, that could change.

Take work by Daron Acemoglu and David Autor of the Massachusetts Institute of Technology, Jonathon Hazell of Princeton University and Pascual Restrepo of Boston University, which was presented at the recent meeting of the American Economic Association (AEA). The authors use rich data provided by Burning Glass Technologies, a software company that maintains and analyses fine-grained job information gleaned from 40,000 firms. They identify tasks and jobs in the dataset that could be done by AI today (and are therefore vulnerable to displacement). Unsurprisingly, the researchers find that businesses that are well-suited to the adoption of AI are indeed hiring people with AI expertise. Since 2010 there has been substantial growth in the number of AI-related job vacancies advertised by firms with lots of AI-vulnerable jobs. At the same time, there has been a sharp decline in these firms' demand for capabilities that compete with those of existing AI.

An AI-induced change in the mix of jobs need not translate into less hiring overall. If new technologies largely assist current workers or boost productivity by enough to spark expansion, then more AI might well go hand-in-hand with more employment. This does not appear to be happening. Instead the authors find that firms with more AI-vulnerable jobs have done much less hiring on net; that was especially the case in 2014-18, when AI-related vacancies in the database surged. But the relationship between greater use of AI and reduced hiring that is present at the firm level does not show up in aggregate data, the authors note. Machines are not yet depressing labour demand across the economy as a whole. As machines become cleverer, however, that could change.

Evidence that AI affects labour markets primarily by taking over human tasks is at odds with some earlier studies of how firms use the technology. A paper from 2019 by Timothy Bresnahan of Stanford University argues that the most valuable applications of AI have nothing to do with displacing humans. Rather, they are examples of "capital deepening", or the accumulation of more and better capital per worker, in very specific contexts, such as the matching algorithms used by Amazon and Google to offer better product recommendations and ads to users. To the extent that AI leads to disruption, it is at a "system level", says Mr Bresnahan—as Amazon's sales displace those of other firms, say.

New work by Ajay Agrawal, Joshua Gans and Avi Goldfarb of the University of Toronto suggests that this state of affairs may not persist for long, though. As the quality of AI predictions improves, they write, it becomes increasingly attractive for AI-using firms to restructure in more radical ways. At some level of accuracy, for example, Amazon's ability to predict consumers' desires could encourage the firm to adjust its business model—by pre-emptively shipping goods to consumers before they ever go searching at Amazon in the first place—in ways that are likely to change how many workers and of what sort the firm requires. In that event, the influence of AI on the economy could change dramatically. So, such as Amazon case, it applies robotics are only concentrated on predicting consumer prediction aspect, AI is only assistant role to Amazon human market researchers. They help Amazon market researchers to gather consumer behavior data , but Amazon human market researchers need to do marketing analysis tasks by themselves. So, Amazon can not employ human market reseachers jobs position in itself company. Amazon needs robotic and human market researchers to do market research tasks in order to achieve how to predict consumer behavior more accurately. Thus, it seems that future large enterprises won't fire any professional staffs more easily because some complex tasks, e.g. analysis tasks, they believe that human's analysis can make more accurate judgement to compare AI's analysis.

However, some scientists believe that some skilful professional occupations , they have possible be replaced by robotic. Will Architects and Engineers be Replaced by Robots? It's not uncommon for people to think they may be replaced by a robot in the workplace. After all, it's happened plenty of times before. For example, the rise of the mechanical assembly line saw machines replace people in the early 20th century. With recent advances in artificial intelligence (A.I.), it's entirely possible that more jobs are at risk. Even skilled workers, such as architects, programmers and engineers may be at risk. One day, an A.I. software developer may be able to do everything that a human programmer can do.

Recent reports have not abated this thought process. In fact, the 2016 Economic Report of the President seemed to suggest that artificial intelligence is playing an increasingly important role in the engineering industry. Just think about the software you use in your work. Many software packages can handle a lot of the complex calculations for you. Yes, this cuts down on the amount of work you do. However, this automation may also present a threat to your job. What if the future sees these same software packages handling data input, as well as processing.

Automation is important. The use of artificial intelligence, alongside various other technologies, has always improved production. More work gets done, which means that businesses make more money. Architects and engineers constantly look for ways to speed up their work. The desire for automation has informed many recent software innovations. Furthermore, project methodologies, like Building Information Modelling, place automation at the fore. That's great for speed and efficiency, but what does it mean for architects and engineers? History has shown that automation has a very human effect. People lose their jobs because machines can do them faster. Just think of it from a business viewpoint. Do you want to pay 10 or more employees, or invest in one machine? More often than not, the machine will cost less than the employees, even if you factor maintenance into the equation. It's a simplification, but not an invalid one. Businesses make these sorts of decisions all the time. By pushing for automation, architects and engineers may be slowly working themselves out of their own jobs.

Several studies have also suggested that artificial intelligence may cause job losses. One recent example comes from the University of Oxford. The study found that over 700 types of jobs are at risk of technological disruption. All told, this means that about 47% percent of jobs are at risk because of artificial intelligence. That is a huge amount of people who may find

themselves obsolete due to advancing technology. The same study also mentioned a concept called the "technological bottleneck". The researchers used this to determine how "at risk" a job was of displacement. The bottleneck takes three factors into account:
•How much creative intelligence the role needs
•If manual manipulation and perception is required
•The role of social intelligence in the role
If a role requires a high degree of any of those three things, it's less likely that it's at risk from artificial intelligence. Architects and engineers are a good example. These professionals require a great deal of creative intelligence. Artificial intelligence and robots may not be able to emulate that creative intelligence. As a result, it's unlikely that architects and engineers need to worry about losing their jobs. Right now, at least. The study concluded with a cautionary note. It said that just because automation enhances an architect and engineer's work right now, it doesn't mean that automation won't replace that role in the future. So, if future human architects or engineers jobs can be replaced to do by robotics. Then, robotic architects can help the architectural firms to design more attractive architectural plans to satisfy construction firms clients needs in short time or robotic engineers can help the engineering design firms to design more attractive machines to satisfy any engineeing customers needs in short time , when robotics can be invented to own excellent creative ability to compare human architects or engineers. So, these two professional occupations will be lost when robotic architects and robotic engineers can be invented to own excellent creative ability to compare human architects or engineer in future one day in possible.
However, robotic architects or engineers may bring advantages and disadvantages both aspects:
On advantages aspect:
Artificial intelligence allows us to do all of the following:
•The completion of mundane tasks that would otherwise take a lot of labour hours. Automating such tasks frees up skilled workers to work on more important tasks.
•A.I. is not as prone to making errors as a person. As long as the A.I.'s programming is good enough, you should find that calculating errors and similar issues become problems of the past.
•Speed is a key feature of artificial intelligence. Huge datasets no longer provide any problems to businesses, as automation allows for much faster

processing. This means that a business can spend money elsewhere.
•The most complex A.I.s reduce the amount of risk attached to the decision-making process. The "Curiosity" Mars rover is a good example. It's programmed to choose the best course of action depending on its position.
On disadvantages aspect:
It's not all good, unfortunately. The following are some of the bad points of artificial intelligence:
•The previously mentioned job losses can cause all sorts of problems for staff morale.
•Some believe that artificial intelligence gets rid of the human element. The nightmare scenarios in films like "The Terminator" may seem far-flung, but that doesn't mean there isn't a risk in letting machines make all the decisions.
•A.I. relies on pre-existing knowledge, which means it lacks creativity. Attempting to use it for creative endeavours may result in failure.
•Algorithms may not be able to make judgement calls in disaster situations. Again, the A.I. may not take the human element into account, no matter what's actually happening on the ground.
Oe people management aspect, what do you think would be the reaction to a robot attempting to manage people? It's likely that a lot of people won't take to kindly to artificial intelligence telling them what to do. Many underestimate the importance of people skills in the architecture and engineering profession. Architects and engineers must be able to organise workloads and manage individuals. It is sure, A.I. device could handle the former. Scheduling is a task that many already automate. However, A.I. will fall down when it comes to the human relationships that are so vital in a team environment. An A.I. won't understand when somebody is demotivated, or why. It won't make allowances for the human issues that affect every problem. This makes skilled team members even more valuable. As A.I. takes an increasing role in the workplace, the need for people management will become more important. Architects and engineers with those skills may even find they make more money to employ them. Although, it is possible that AI can replace human architects or engineers to do their tasks to be better , it can help any one architectural or enginering firms to improve design performace in order to satisfy customers design demand, but our societies will increase unemployment ratio to engineers and architects number, even universities will reduce architect and engineering students number. Our traditional professional knowledge will

be felt to be rubblish when these professional subjects won't be useful to help us to find jobs easily. So, AI invention will influence many students won't choose to study these two subjects. Our societies will be influence to experience knowledge recession when knowledge will become rubblish because robotics invention , it can do many human professional jobs to do. " knowledge recession" will be important factor to bring economic recession, because human can not be encouraged to learn any new knowledge to prepare to enter job market due to robotic invention can replace us to do more complex tasks in our future societies.

Can robotic leadership be good solution method when recession had come to the country?

On leadership management aspect, can robots become clever leadership to any organizations? As artificial intelligence becomes further embedded into our everyday working lives, we are already seeing the footprint of machine learning, automation, algorithms and robots in many of our professions and sectors. However, when we look at the upper levels of business management and leadership, these technological shifts are less evident, with C level Executives continuing to lead and strategise as they have done before. In Ireland, there are more than 500 CEOs. The question is, when will we start to see machines and robots play a more central role in the CEO sphere, and is a 'Robot CEO' realistic in the short to medium term?

New research shows that 24% of people aged 25-29 would replace their boss with a robot, demonstrating an interesting trend among Generation Z. However, these data sets are perhaps less founded in AI and robotics and more in current employee engagement. It's telling that the 20-30% of people who would willingly replace their human boss with a robot is about the same percentage of people who are consistently classified as "actively disengaged" at work. In addition, research from analytics giant Gallup demonstrates that 70% of how we feel about work, namely our emotional commitment, is driven by who our manager is, again underlining the centrality of human behavioural traits when making decisions on leadership.

As the Irish economy moves forward, values will define how we use and leverage the potential of AI. Tomo Noda of the Harvard Business Review believes that we will need more focus on leadership with humanity, ethics and integrity, stating "only good people can create good AI."With many roadblocks and challenges for the economy looming, primarily in the shape of Brexit and trade tariffs, it is a sound integration of both human and tech which will provide the leadership required to ensure our economy remains robust. Human leaders have played a central role in helping to steer us out of the 2008 recession, and with diplomacy and relationship building key to our post-Brexit future, humans will undoubtedly be the key influencers within the C level for decades to come. Hence, it seems that future organizations ought choose to apply robots to assist leaders to do make important decision, if robotics can assist leaders to make any important decision to conclude the best results to improve any companies performance. Then, GDP may be influenced to increase or grow rapidly, when recession had come to the country. So, robotic leadership may be one solution to solve recession method in possible.

The Recession Cometh and Robots are Ready

In economic demand vs. supply theory indicates that consumer appetites for customized product and their expectations for ever-lowering costs. So the current tug-of-war over if, when, and where a recession will hit is not unchartered territory. For manufacturers, though, the uncertainty is particularly challenging, as the flexibility that allows operations to reflect the pace of the economy simply isn't there. The economy has been growing. Unemployment is down. Last year's Christmas sales were better than they've been in a long time. All good and logical reasons for manufacturers to hire.

Recently though, there have been signs that instability is coming. The US stock market experienced extreme volatility as 2018 came to a close. The Federal Reserve raised interest rates and laid down some pretty clear language that more was to come. Consumer confidence fell. In the UK, a deal on Brexit that would allow British manufacturers to continue to do business with the EU seemed elusive at best. The Chinese government announced that growth in its economy has slowed. And the "R" word started to appear with more frequency. These are not signs that inspire confidence. So, manufacturers once again find themselves in a place they know so well. The rock: the need to hire workers to keep ahead of demand. Compounding this challenge is that unemployment is low and it is very hard to find people with the skills needed to take a job in manufacturing and be ready to work on day one. The hard place: overwhelmingly, today's automation is fixed, expensive, and able to perform only a single task.

As one supply chain executive of a global automotive firm shared recently, "In a downturn...it is about flexibility. All of the automation we have cost too much and it is too complicated to change what it does. What we need is flexible automation that can respond when and how we need it to."Can robotics be applied to manufacturing industry to avoid cost reduces to manufacturers when consumption number reduces or recession is coming? So what makes the most sense? Hire, hoping that if and when recession comes, it will be short-lived and you won't have to lay folks off? Or try to invest in reconfiguring existing automation?

Hence, cobots give manufacturers the flexibility they need to thrive in good times and not-so-good times. Advances in robotic technology make it possible to put cobots to work

•at lower costs

•on more than a single task

•in the same amount of time, it takes to train a person – or even less

With collaborative robots, manufacturers can build the operations they need to compete and thrive regardless of the economic climate, where manufacturing robotic participation can help organizations to reduce labours number on strategic tasks and flexibility is part of the organizational human resource cost reducing strategy. It seems that robotic manufacturing workers can help organizations to reduce manufacturing cost when recession is coming. Consequently, these applying manufacturing robotic businesses may prolong business life time in possible. So, it seems that manufacturing robots may help organizations to reduce manufacturing cost to keep life when recession is coming.

● How non-manual driving public transport influences public transport drivers number reduces

It has close relationship between globalization and global tranport development. How globalisation impacts on the environment via changes taking place in the transport sectors. In fact, it is not clear how the relative price changes that result from openness will affect the environental composition of economic activity. For example, some countries will produce more environmentally intensive goods, others will produce fewer. On the other hand, liberalisation will raise incomes, perhaps increasing the willingness to pay for environmental improvement. These potential income effects increased outweigh the negative scale effects with increased economic activities. When combined with the positive effects with technology transfer, the net effect on local pollutants could be positive . Hence, we need to find methods to solve the problem of raising transport economic activities and serious environmental pollution creating as the same time occurrence.

Globalisation helps to facilitate greater division of labor, and to exploit its comparative advantage more completely. In longer term, globalization also stimilates technology an dlabour transfers, and allows the dynamism that accompanies economic activities to stimulate the development of new transport technologies and short time transport processes that lead to global welfare improvement.

On shipping transport industry aspect, shipping will increase ocean pollution, when international shipping activities are increasing. Trade and shipping encourages energy use in shipping is coupled with the movement of waterborne commerce. The estimates depending on the transport goods number of at-sea or in port days much increase globally every day. The energy demand of international shipping fuel sale number and domestically assigned fuel sales number also increases for global fuel usage. Estimates of ocean going ships now consume about 2% to 3% and perhaps even as much as 4% of world fossil fuels.Hence, when global shipping energy fuel usage number increases, because global shipping trading activities number increases. It will bring the environmental pollution to ocean level increases.

On air transport industry aspect, their travellers' catching air plans travelling needs and businesses' goods transport air delivery service needs are increasing from the requirements for high quality , fast and reliable international transport. Moreover, the networks that airline companies operate have changed often to hub-and spoke networks, many new often low -cost companies have entered the air freight market, any long time air journey is needed, e.g. Australia airline expands its one new air journey flies to UK, it needs two days flying time. It means that every flight to UK from Australia , it needs to use more fuel to fly. Then , air pollution will increase also.

On road transport industry aspect, global road transport cost and transit times, traffic jam occurrence chances also increase because when the road building number is increasing globally. So, it will cause traffic jam and long journey time spending , even fuel usage spending number is also increased. Then, accident occurrence chance is raised. Hence, global business or entertainment transport activities number increasing , it will bring much negative impact on environmental pollution, traffic jams number increases, long journey spending time increases, fuel usage number increases. Although , frequent transport activities may bring GDP income.

On transport service industy aspect, but is also brings negative influence to standard of living. It means that when transport fuel demand increases, transport activities number increases, GDP income on relative any transport activities needs industy , e.g. logistic demand needs, when lorry drivers need to drive lorries to deliver goods from one warehouse to another warehouse or supermarket or office etc. different business places on the road driving activities increase. But, it also bring air pollution , traffic noise and traffic jam etc. transport problems to road and natural environment and raises worse standard of living , bad emotion to working people or learning emotion to students , due to frequent traffic jam causes , low efficiency and productivity to workers, even student individual learning time can be reduced if they need to spend long time to wait bus, ferry, rail, underground train to go to schools , due to frequent long time traffic jam occurs on the roads to influence they can not go to schools on time often when they are catching buses to go to schools absolutely in busy transport time.

Thus, although any countries need to consider how to design their transport system, e.g. how to e.g. how to choose the right locations to build roads to let many cars can be driven available easily when the morning and evening (office and school transport busy time, e.g. 6:00 to 9:00 AM morning, 6:00 to 9:00 PM in the evening transport time usually because these two transport periods are usually , there are many students and working people need to catch any public transportation or drive cars tools to go back homes. So, enough roads number and long and not narrow road area must be needed to design in order to let enough cars be driven on the roads in the transport busy times to the countries have many big cities or have high population , such as UK, US, China, India, Hong Kong. They have many people , but drivers and cars numbers both are increasing. So, efficient road design and road number are also needed to increase in order to let drivers can transport goods to deliver, students and working people can catch any public transport tools to arrive any destinations on reads in the short time rapidly in order to avoid to spend long time transportation time and late to arrive any destinations in possible occurrence. So, any sudden traffic jam is not hoped to be caused by easy traffic accidents occurrence any time.

Hence, global efficient road transport system is needed, when global transport activities are increased, because any road logistic transport activities are increasing, they will also influence the students and working people when they also need to catch any public transport tools or drive themselves cars to go to working places or schools on the roads at the same busy transport time between 6:00 to 9:00 AM morning busy transport time and between 6:00 to 9:00 PM evening busy transport time. Because these both times will be have many students, working people , they need either go to offices or schools or go to homes. Hence, if the country had many lorry drivers need to drive their lorries to deliver goods on the roads in the transport busy morning or evening time in the same driving time on the roads. It will increase the risk to cause frequent traffic jam or traffic accident occurrence easily in possible in the country. So, any countries' governments can not neglect how to design roads and choose anywhere are the roads suitable locations to be built as well as anywhere land useful number to build road location choices in order to solve geographical traffic jams occurrence chance.

Hence, globalization of transport activities may bring geographical GDP growth, but it also bring traffic jams and traffic accidents occurrences, hearing impairment due to traffic noise, air pollution, traffic crashed, bad working emotions to workers and bad learning emotions to students, due to spending long transport time when traffic jam or traffic accidence occurs more easily.

However, transportation is an important tool if a country's progress. Rapid economic growth and increasing level of urbanization enhances a person's living standard have, it leads to a greater travel demands. Hence, governments ought not neglect have to design its roads , measure every road's length or width whether it has how many cars need to drive in morning or evening transport busy time for students, working people and delivery goods drivers of public transportation tools or private transportation tools easy driving needs in order to avoid frequent traffic jams or traffic accidents occurrences in possible.

Moreover, any governments also need to solve these issues, if they hope to develop their transport system successfully. These issues include : What mode of transportation to cost-effective in meeting a region's transportation needs to the country? How should a state department of transportation prioritize its highway delivers to maximize economic growth? What is the trade-off between additional growth in urban area and the cost of expanding transportation systems to accommodate greater growth? What effect does the expansion of transportation systems have on the need to invest in other types of transport modes? For example , the transport expansion may include the construction of additional highway segments, rail lines, runways, or additional sea, air, rail or bus terminal capacity using traditional technology; highway may include the additional of lanes to an interstate highway system; the conversion of an existing two-lane road to a four lane limited access highway, replacement or widening of bridges, and the extension of an existing road. Airport examples, include runway lengthening, apron expansion, and additional terminal gates.

On the other hand, enhancement to new transport technologies may bring efficiency of the existing highway system, examples may include intelligent highway systems, congestion pricing, intermodal freight facilities, geographic positioning systems, and instrument landing systems to mention of a few major transport innovations. So, transport policy makers need to understand the effects of these new transport mode innovations on economic development or GDP growth on transport activities growth transportation services and a more efficient use of limited land supplying scarce resources , air quality ,and noise pollution, traffic jams, long spending transport time to students, working people, entertaining people, even deliver goods lorry drivers their every day essential driving activities or catching public transportation tools needs problems. For example, the concept of intelligent highway systems needs increase trend. In simply , vehicles are being linked to each other and to traffic control devices to improve the efficiency of the total highway system. Similar types of innovations in intelligent traffic management are increasing needs for air, sea, and rail systems. The question is that whether intelligent highway systems can attribute of highways on economic development, raising on productivity of reducing highway congestion or improving pavement condition.

In fact, many developed countries' transportation system is mature. The nation has gone beyond the frontier of building, the interstate highway system and connecting most cities (markets). Tweaking the system with additional lanes and the new intelligent highway systems are useful in China, US, UK, because they have many cities. SO, road efficient traffic congestion control is needed when many students, working people, delivery goods transport people need to drive cars or catch cars on every city's roads in the transport busy time between 6:00 to 9:00 AM morning transport busy time as well as between 6:00 to 9:00 PM evening transport busy time.

However, transportation investment must be needed, if the country hoped to have good economic productivity, efficient transport service can bring good effects on the flows goods and people on roads every day when they use the country's transport system. So, any countries need to collect data, they can not be lack of enough transport information in any time that links anywhere locations of any drivers to the locations of the transport system that provide them with services in any time, e.g. every day morning and evening transport busy time, radio can report the real transport time of any roads traffic jam or traffic accident message to let drivers to listen to know whether anywhere roads are occurring traffic accidents or traffic jams or when the road traffic accident or traffic jam is solved to let the drivers can know whether when the roads can be opened to drive again. So, real time road transport message information is needed to report by radio, in order to let any drivers to know whether they ought choose to drive themselves cars on the road when they need to choose anywhere road to drive to the destination if they can know when the road has traffic accident or traffic jam occurs. They won't drive their cars on the road in the moment immediately.

On conclusion, globalization can being frequent transport economic activities. So, road , air, sea, transport service users' transport service needs are also increased. Every country ought not neglect how to innovate their transport service in order to satisfy their transport needs to achieve economic growth, efficient and short transport time spending, productivities increase, reducing air pollution, traffic noise , raisins standard of living on transport influence aspect to satisfy working people, students, entertaining people, delivery goods transport users' efficient road transport time behavioral spending aspect.

Artificial intelligent public transport how influences passenger psychology

How technology influence passenger psychology

Nowadays, robotic invention can be applied to factory manufacture, hotel, restaurant, shopping center, customer service, accounting, law document draft etc. general office tasks aspect, evem hospital surgen patient medical operation health service aspects. If future robotic non -manual driving vehicles can be invented to reach the safe auto driving mature skill stage. Any one driver begins to believe robotic, driving safe level is bette than he/she drives himself/herself car. I assume that if future robotic public transport tool drivers can replace human public transport tool drivers to drive bus, taxi, train, tram, ferry, underground train, tram , even air plane ets. different kinds of public transport tools. How non maual driving public transport tools influence our social change either to improve better ot worse? How non manual driving public transport tools influence passenger psychology, e.g. increasing any kinds of public transport tools passengers safe feeling to choose to catch any kinds of public transport tools to go to anywhere or feeling more dangerous when the passenger himself/herself chooses to sit the non manual driving public transport tool.

In past, traditional public transport tools are driven by human drivers, if one day non manual driving skills are invented to reach the most safe level, when the car owner or passenger is sitting on the non manual driving vehicle or public transport tool, the artificial intelligent driver can help the driver to control the car wheel to avoid to crash any other cars or pedestrians to o to any far places on the roads easily. The public bus does not human driver to drive the bus, artificial intelligent driver won't feel tried, when it drives the bus long time, it does not need to leave the bus to go to toilet, to go to restaurant to eat, to go to rest room for rest, because it is one (AI) machine. So, the (AI) driver won't have negative emotion to feel angry when the bus passenger complaints its service is poor when he feels dissatisfactory to the (AI) driver bus service performance.

However, human bus driver may be complainted for unpolite or rude bus service attitude. It is common human bus driver will encounter any unreasonable passenger complain in general . Hence, when non manual driving technology can be invented to reach the most safe driving skill level, whether (AI) machine driver is the most suitable to replace any public transport tool drivers, such as bus, taxi, train, underground train, ferry, tram, even air plane to drive for future passengers service need.

In fact, any public transport tool drivers may cause traffic transport accidents, due to their careless driving to crash any other vehicles or pedestrians (walling people). Consequently, any passengers may have chance to be killed by public transport tool crashing accident. So, it seems that global public transport tools are dangerous to any passengers, when they are sitting on the bus, taxi, train, tram, underground train road public transport tools, or ferry sea public transport tools, because any human public transport tool drivers will feel tried to drive any one kind of public transport tool long time, for example when the bus driver has no enough nervous to drive the bus, he wants to sleep, due to he often needs to follow night time bus timetable to drive bus long time at night. When he often want to sleep and he is driving the bus, traffic accidents will be caused easily. So, any passenger individual life is dominated by the sleeping bus driver. His bus dirving behavior is not safe to any one bus passenger when the bus passegner chooses to catch this feeling sleeping bus driver's bus to catch.
Otherwise, (AI) non manual driver must not feel tried or need sleep often.

It is one automative driving mature, it can drive any kinds of public transport tools all day, because (AI) machine drivers do not need sleep, (AI) none human auto-driving driver can bring this important unique benefit to any kinds of public transport tools to compare human drivers. Instead of (AI) automatic driving tools' non need sleeping advantage, (AI) non-manual control auto-driving tools must not own sad, disappointing feeling , tried feeling, anygry emotion feeling when it needs to contact angry passengers every day. So, I mean that any traffic accident occurrence will reduce, when (AI) drivers often feel happy to drive any kinds of public transport tools. Otherwise, any human public transport drivers will be influenced to feel angry when they are complaint by angry passenger in any driving time easily. So, public transport traffic accident will be caused to occur easily. Althoug, it is not guarantee that it is obsolute none any public transport accident occurrence, due to crash to other vehicles, during the non manual driving (AI) driver drives the bus, tram, train, taxi, on the road, nut when (AI) non manual driving skill can be improved to the most safe driving level. I believe that non manual driving public transport tools ought be bring more safe to compare human public transport tools drivers to any one passenger individual life safety.

How non manual driving automated vehicle influences future mode of public transport service change? A survey distributed in the Netherlands in which respondents had to choose between conventional cars, public transportation for different travel distances and trip purposes. having collected information from 663 respondents, conducted a study on classic trip attributes (such as travel time, car owner self driving time and non manual driving public transport tool driving time as well as travel costs, car owner car fuel purchase expenditure and general non manual driving public transport tool fare comparison), attitudinal factors and socio-economic variables to understand future non manual auto driving public transport tools choices. The repor indicates that automated driving transport service which they defined as an automatically controlles door-to-door transport service provided by a vehicle with similar features to a conventional car, albeit driveless. Results suggest that travellers' mode preferences vary significantly for different travel distances and purposes. They found that conventional cars and public transportation are perceived as being the least attraction altererernatives in relation to vehicle travel time and short -and -long distance commuting trips respectively, preference for passegner choice is between the non-manual driving auto car and non manual driving auto public transport tool.

They indicated that future passengers will consider how non-manual driving public transport tools whether they can bring trips are safer, faster and more efficient to let them to feel as well as traveling time and time cost is also another factor to influence them to choose to catch non-manual driving public transport tool, when they feel safe to arrive the destination rapidly. Then, future many passengers will be persuaded to choose to catch non-manual auto driving public transport tools in preference. So, if future all public transport service providers can let passengers to feel fares are reasonable price, when their non-manual driving public service transport tools, bus, taxi, tram, train, underground train etc. they can let them to feel safe to arrive destinations rapidly, they won't need worry about passengers number will reduce when human drivers are replaced by AI robotic drivers. In fact, when one needs to drive to arrive destination in long driving time. The car owner will feel tried, bored and he/she can not spend driving time to do his/her interesting activites in his/her car, e.g. reading, listening music, watching TV, playing electronic games from smartphone, phone talking etc. personal behaviors. So, it means that future long time trip passengers may be persuaded to catch non-manual auto driving public transport tools if they believe that this kind of new non manual auto driving pubic transport tools can provide more safe, efficient, rapid, comfortable feeling to them, when they are sitting on them.

All of these may be the main factors to influence them to choose to catch non -manual auto driving public transport tools. In general, these other factors may influence future passengers to choose to catch non manual auto driving public transport tools, they may include: whether automated vehicle would drive on populated streets better than conventional cars, whether an automated car would be comfortable entrusting the safety of a close family member, whether automated vehicle might produce fewer pollutant emissions. Because , when future non-manual auto driving vehicles are popular, many car owners will choose to buy automated vehicles to drive. So, future non manual auto driving public transport tool service providers , their competitors may be automated vehicles. If automated vehicles can let car owners to feel car prices are reasonable, they can provide safe, rapid speed, comfortable feeling to any one car owner, then he/she can sell his/her traditional car to change new automated car easily, when global many car owners begin to accept automated cars.

On conclusion, future passengers may be persuaded to choose to buy fares to catch any kinds of non manual auto driving public transportation tools. It depends on these factors, such as reasonable fares, safe feeling, efficient and rapid arriving to destinations short time journey, comfortable and clean seats facility, free personal behavior, e.g. quite reading , listening music, watching TV , free internet provision transport environment, when future any one passenger is sitting in the auto driving public transport vehicle. So, (AI) technology will have possible to influence our future social public transportation development may bring more significant new travelling experiences and it can let global passengers to feel indeed. Moreover, it will be future global public transportation service providers, they need to consider that they ought need to change their public transport tools services in order to satisfy future passengers transport needs more easily. I conclude that future global public transport service will be influenced to change non manual auto driving public transport services by future global passegner public transport service needs within 10 years. So, nowadays, any kinds of public transport service providers ought need to spend time to research how to design themselves traditional public transport service moods to change to non manual auto driving moods in order to satisfy future global passenger individual new public transport services needs successfully.

Hence, (AI) driving machine learning system can be applied to road driving skill aspect. When intelligent vehicles are invented to own the most safe driving judgement skill and they can know when either they may auto drive fast speed, when they are feeling to know when there are not many vehicles are moving close/near to them or when they need auto drive slow speed, when they are feeling to know when there are many vehicles are moving close/ near to them. Then driving consumers will have more confidence to choose to buy any kinds of intelligent vehicles to replace manual driving vehicles to drive on the roads.

● Non-manual driving transportation tool market development

Future Human Transport Need Change

How future our transport need change? What factors influence our future transport need change? In general, these factors may influence our transportation need change. They may include fuel cost, the labor market for commercial drivers, demand for frieight , customer loyalty , vehicle capacity, government regulation, geographical events, the public transport tool reputation to passengers as a merchant. However, the factors that influence the development of transport system in an area? They may include as below:

Environment at the local scale existing hydrographical and geomorphological characteristics are string, factors in transport development, particularly in terms of the technical challenges (bridge, gradients,) they present to construct, other factors may include historical, technological, political and economic factors. All of these factors may influence our future transport system how develops. For raiway development influential factors, they may include: Geograohical factors, e.g. the North Indian plain with its level land, high density of population and rich agriculture presents the most favourable conditions for the development of railways in India. However, the presence of large number of rivers makes it necessary to construct bridges which involve heavy expenditure to Indian Government publich transport expenditure.

How transport has changed from past to present?

There has been a remarkable development in modern transportation. The stream engine and then the stream trains have emerged and spread at this time and in abundance until the discovery of natural gas and oil was an evolution of transportation. Thus, the sedams and vehicles began to run in oil, until present battery changes energy vehicle need, even future non-manual driving artificial intelligent driving vehicle need. These new transport technology may influence our future public transportation from gas energy to battery changed energy, even non-manual driving vehicles need to our daily transport need.

So, our future purpose of public transport need is the unique purpose to oversome space, which is shaped by a variety of human and physical constraints, such as distance, time. These both is our future main public transport need main purpose factors, short distance and reducing journey time, they influence that why we need to choose to catch any kinds of public transportation tool to replace purchase private cars to drive transport tool choice. So, future any kinds of public transport tools, they need to consider above both main factors , how to attract passengers to choose to catch themselves public transport tools choice in this competitive public transport tools market.

On the other hand, the economic importance of transportation development can be defined as improving the welfare of a society, through appropriate social, political and economic conditions , such as US Government spent too much money to assist MTR (MAss transport railway firm) to develop underground thrain transport. Its aim to let many passegner can reduce journey time and reduce distance between destinations, it also hopes US citizen passengers can pay cheap transport fare to buy ticket to catch underground transport train for many families their transport expenditure in social transport welfare view.

However, US Government neds to solve those challenges, before it implements to develop rapid underground railway , e.g. lack of knowledge of geographical fwatures, lack of manpower necessary to operate the rapid underground railway construction work, lack of construction materials within the US itself. For Brazil rail network transportation development example, the factors influence the use of rail network for transportion is highly restricted in Brazil. Thus, the development of roadways and waterways is the main modes of transportation that caould be used in Brazil given its topography and drainage benefit to society . So, brazil can develop rail network for transportation development in success.

So, transportation system is important in the development of any nation, because transportation plays important role in rapid economic growth of a nation. Thrapsortation increases the quality and variety of consumer goods, thereby stimulating the demand and development of trade and economy of the nation. Moreover, transport provides various employment opportunities and boosts up the economy of the country.

Also, any transport tools need to improve themselves transport service in order to attract passengers to choose their public transport service more easily. They may attempt to sign up for an autonomous vehicle pilot program, free phone enquiey concerns whether the passegner can catch which bus bumber to go to the destination, hou much bus fare, how long journey time, when the bus will arrive teh bus stops or leave the bus stop etc. bus service questions, before any one passenger prepares to choose to catch bus (free bus go phone call enquiry), free download a public transport tool transit app. even water taxi tranport tool innovation can replace ferry public transport tool, it can let passengers have more fun an enjoyable catching feeling. So, water taxi tranport tool is one kind of future new transport tool change to replace ferry , it can influence ferry passengers to choose water taxi public transport tool to replace ferry. Although, its fare may be more expsnse to compare ferry, but it can reduce jounrey time and distance between both water stations, when ferry can not arrive the other destinations, but water taxi can arrive any one water station destination. It can bring convenient to future any one ferry passengers. So, water taxi may be developed to some countries, e.g. New Zealand , Auckland city, US , Washington and New York cities they had developed water taxi public transport tools to let ferry passengers have one kind new water public transport choice.

However, instead of new transport innovation improvement to water transport service public transport with input from the public on bus transport service aspect, bus frequency improvement, it means when booking at ways to improve, bus frequency from long times to less times, efficient bus ticketing system, a big part of how to improve tranportation efficiency is improving transit ticketing system.

In fact, my future transport system may still include these five types, modes of transport are: railway, roadways, airways, waterways and piplelines. Also, among different includes of transport, railways are the different modes of transport, railways are the cheapest. Trains cover the distance in less time and comparatively, the fare is also less to other modes of transporation. Therefore, railways is the cheapest mode of transportation to compare ferry, water taxi , sea transport, bus, taxi, road system.

On conclusion, transport price is not the main factor to attract passegners to choose to catch. The importance to have a good public transport system in place. It may be one main factor to help the kind of public transport tool to attract passengers to choose to catch, because a good transport links can widen people's job search area and help them find employment. It can also reduce commuting times and reduce the cost of living, and high skilled workers are more likely to travel across longer distances to work, especially if they are following good job opportunities. So, future any one kind of public transportation tool service provider ought consider how to satisfy working people working time need to shorten journey time to any working places or student learning time need to shorten jounrey times to any schools as well as let they feel comfortable to sit on comfortable chairs or provide free internet service to themselves mobiles , laptops, when they are sitting down or standing up in the kind of public transport . It is the important factor to influence any kind of public transport service in success.

Future Non-Manual driving vehicle How
Influences Public Transport Tool Passenger Need

Nowadays, artifical intelligent (non-manual) driving vehicles are invented, it may be accepted to any countries families to feel comfortable to drive on roads, because any people choose to buy any kinds cars, when any people choose to buy kinds of non-manual (artificial intelligent) vehicles, they do not need to use their hands to drive cars, because artificial intelligent (robotic auto control wheels, it means that robots can help human (drivers) to control wheel to drive to avoid any cars crash occurrence on the roads more easily.

If one day, non-manual driving robotic control whoole vehicles are invented in successful, whether it will persuade many different conuntries families choose to buy non-manual (robotic auto control wheel) vehicles, then it will cause bus, tram, train, underground train, road transport need will be influenced to reduce or even if non-manula boats are invented, whether it will cause ferry sea transport needs will b influenced to reduce. Hence, future non-manual driving vehicles or bats invention whether they will influence public transport tool of road and sea transport passengers number reduces. It is one interesting question. I shall attempt to discuss as below:

In fact, non-manual vehicles are very attraction, to excite any person chooses to buy to drive, because people do not need often touch wheels and touch foots button to control cars to move often forever, when robotic can be invented to help human to control car wheel and foot button, any person only needs to sit on his/her car, then the car can move rapidly, because any drivers is lazy, he/she hopes machine can help her/him to drive car on the road safely. So, he/she can read book or listen music or eatch mobile movie to enjoy his/her entertainment when he/she is sitting on his/her car.He/she will feel more comfortable and enjoyable when robotic can help him/her to drive car. So, robotic (non -manual driving vehicle) can encourage people to choose to buy cars because any drivers won't need to drive cars, robotic can help drivers them to drive on the road easily, when global any one family can own one robotic auto control (non-manual driving) car at least, it may influence these owning non-manula diriving vehicle owners do not feel need to pay any fares to buy road public transport tools of bus ticket, train ticket, underground train ticket , tram ticket to go to anywhere. So, it seems that robotic (non-manual driving) vehicles may influence future any road transport passengers number reduces , because traditional catching any kinds of road public transport tool passengers will be influenced to choose to sit themselves auto (non-manual) driving cars to go to offices to work, parents do not need to follow their sone/daughters to sit on themselves non-manual auto driving cars to go to schools, because their sons/daughters can sit on themselves non-manual driving cars to go to schools more easily. In holidays, they can sit on themselves non-manual driving cars to go to cinemas, music halls, breachs, theaters, shopping centers, gardens different entertainment places to enjoy their any leisure safely because robotic can help them to drive their cars on roads safely.

So, it means that robotic auto control driving cars can influence global every family to feel that they do not need to catch any kinds of public transport tools, e.g. bus, train, tram, taxi underground train to go to anywhere because robotic auto driving cars can help any one, he/she does not know how to drive car to go to anywhere safely. So, future any one won't need to learn driving car skill, when he/she likes to buy one auto driving car. So, in passenger public transport need view, non-manual driving cars will influence them to feel any kinds of road public transport tools can help them to go to anywhere conveniently, because themselves non-manual driving vehicles can help them to drive cars to go to anywhere conveniently. They only need to tell robotic that where they want to go, when they sit on their non-manual driving cars, then robotic knows whether where destination, they want to go, their cars will auto move on the road immediately. It is one exciting and enjoyable ourney when the driver does not need to drive his/her car on the road. So, it seems that robotic (non-manual driving) vehicles invention may bring negative influence to any kinds of public transport tools service needs to passengers , when passengers had owned one non-manual driving car at least.

If Non-manual driving vehicle manufacturers expect their (AI) automatic vehicles can attract drivers to buy. I feel them to need to consider how (AI) driving machine learning system can achieve these requirements in order to satisfy manual driving vehicle drivers‘ requirement to change their traditional driving habit to choose non-manual driving needs. It means (AI) driving machine learning systems can help them to drive vehicles to replace manual driving vehicles on the road. This is the main factor to influence car buyers choose to buy intelligence driving vehicles replace to manual driving vehicles. I believe (AI) non-manual driving vehicle machine learning systems, need to be designed as below:

(1) Improving driving safety by preventing accidents from happening.

Every year, drivers are facing a large number of casualties, due to traffic accidents. The amount of killed and injured road traffic related accidents is increasing every year. The real cost of an accident can go well beyond the limits of immediate material destruction, and is impossible to evaluate.
Hence, researchers and car manufacturers are looking for solutions in order to reduce the amount of accidents. They already developed a considerable set of technologies in order to decrease the amount of casualties. Most of them (like airbags, seat-belts, anti-lock systems, shock absorbing car bodies) are efficient in decreasing the impact of an accident, and in protecting the passengers of the cars. The technologies already saved a lot of lives, but they are rarely able to avoid accidents because they do not anticipate them. Moreover, if they are protecting in many cases, the passengers of the car, they do not prevent most traffic participants, like pedestrians on bicyclists from getting injured. it causes (AI) non-manual automatic car manufacturers need to consider how to design machine learning safety system is to prevent accident from happening instead of just reducing their impact.
This can only be possible using intelligent systems that can observe the driving environment, reason and decide if there is a danger, determine how to avoid it and act if necessary

(2) Reducing energy consumption by optimizing the driving.
Nowadays, global air pollution is serious. (AI) non-manual driving car manufacturers need to concern how to design (AI) machine learning system can reduce degree of air pollution to be the most minimum level to compare to traditional manual driving vehicles.
The reduction of energy consumption if certainly one of the main challenges. Transportation is one of the major factors in fossil energy consumption, and it is also responsible for a large amount of CO2 pollution. It is difficult to ask individuals to voluntarily limit the use of their vehicle of they do not have a strong incentive to do so. Specially in regions where vehicles are needed to drive to go to work every day. It stands to reason that if it is difficult to decrease the amount of vehicles, part of the solution is to make them more energy efficient.
Hence, non-manual driving car manufacturers need to design how to improve engines, which are more optimized and need less fuel to operate, and hybrid and electric cars have been developed and are continuously being improved. But we can go beyond these solutions that do not take into account the environment in which a vehicle is driving. A growing

number of scientific contributions presented intelligent systems used in order to improve energy efficiency and reduce fuel consumption, based on the optimization of the way (AI) non-manual driving (AI) vehicles are performing. Such as recharge batteries and electric engine will be predicted the popular fuel in order to limit fuel consumption to future (AI) non-manual driving vehicles. They can reduce air pollution, consume less fuel for (AI) non-manual driving vehicles.

(3) Improving comfort by anticipating (AI) non- manual driving vehicle drivers.

Finally, another application for intelligent vehicle is the improvement of driving comfort. Car industry is very competitive market. Many potentials (AI) intelligent vehicle customers need to enjoy to sit more comfortable intelligent vehicles, who will be attracted by (AI) comfortable systems improving when driving, so part of the research in intelligent systems from cars focuses on how to improve the driving experience, i.e. make it easier and more enjoyable, more comfortable to compare to traditional manual driving vehicles.

As an example, lane keeping assistant systems are technologies that actively keep the vehicle in the lane in highways of the driven drifts out of it. Automatic speed regulation keeps the car at a certain speed without requiring to touch the gas pedal. This can be really interesting for, e.g. (AI) non-manual driving truck drivers that spend a lot of time on highways. But these technologies have a limitation in the case of automatic speed regulation, this technology can not copy of a vehicle ahead drives slower than the desired speed, or if another vehicle cuts into the lane.

This case requires the driver to have a constant focus on the road. In order to achieve more comfort, it is better of the system can adapt to changes in its dynamic environment: let the (AI) intelligent vehicle adapt to the speed of the man-manual vehicle, or autonomously change lane when requires. Again, this requires knowledge about the environment, detection capabilities, reasoning and action planning. Intelligent systems can be used in order to create more attractive and more comfortable and more safe, less energy consumption and less fuel expenditure by intelligent vehicles.

So, any non-manual driving auto car buyers must need to believe (AI) non-manual driving vehicles (ML) systems can make accurate driving judgement to reduce or avoid any traffic accident occurrences more than human drivers' driving judgement when the (ML) systems are driving their cars on the roads. Then the intelligent vehicle manufacturers will have possible to sell their non-manual driving vehicles success.

This is the first reason or idea influences consumer individual choice to buy any kinds of (AI) non-manual driving vehicles, when consumers believe (ML) systems are more safe and make more accurate judgement to compare human or computer systems, when they are sitting in one non-manual auto driving vehicle on the road.

The another second reason or idea is that some common limits on driving consumer prediction might be understood as the kinds of errors made by poor implementation of machine learning.

Supposing driving consumers believe (AI) machine learning ability is worse to compare to human learning ability. It will also influence driving consumers do not accept to use any (AI) non-manual auto driving vehicles to replace every driver is essential on driving by himself/herself on the road. The third idea or reason is that it is important to influence driving customers believe how (AI) non-manual auto driving technology is used in them can both overcome and exploit human driving skill and safe limits and raise more auto driving safe judgement to compare human driving safe judgement.

However, how to predict any kinds of (AI) non-manual driving vehicles future consumption effort, due to different kinds of (AI) non-manual driving transportation vehicles which have different unique functions and designs to be used by different kinds of road transportation or driving demand of consumers. For example, lorry drivers need non-manual intelligent system can help them to drive fast, but safe to assist them to transport cargo to arrive destinations from their factories or offices. Otherwise, private car driver expects whose (AI) non-manual driving vehicle can auto drive to send to whom to arrive destination in safe way and non-too fast and non-too slow speed in order to avoid accident occurrences.

- How non human driving behavior can be influence by non-manual driving cars

In fact, impact of automated vehicless on travel mode preference, it can bring both trip purposes and distances aim raising need to any kinds of public transport service passegners. Because of technology penetration in the transportation system, the automated vehicle is set to be a future mode of transport, it may bring negative impact to future any kinds of public transport passengers needs, in special on the potential impact of these non-manual driving automated vehicles on travel behaior negative impact to public transport passenger behavior. Automated vehicles will influence future public transportation passengers feel it can bring more short time travel distances and short trip purposes more benefit than any kinds of public transport choices, e.g. bus, taxi, ferry, train, tram, underground tram etc. road and sea public transport tools, e.g. ferry, water taxi. It means that when future any passenger feels above these any one kind of public transport tool needs to spend longer travel time on journey distance and trip to compare future automated vehicles, then they will choose to sit on automated vehicles in preference, due to automated vehicles can help global any one person needs to go to anywhere rapidly.

So, automated vehicles may replace general traditional public transport tools in possible, when they are popular accepted in societies. On the other, instead of shortening journey travel distance time, (travel time) aspect, public transport fare, travel cost will be another influential factor to influence future public transport tool passengers to choose automated vehicles to replace to catch any kinds of public transport tools.

In fact, conventional cars and public transport s are perceivd as being the least attractive alternative in relation to in-vehicle travel time on short and long distance communting trips. So , future automated vehicle drivers (non -human driving) behaviors will be likely changed to prefer this mode for long distance leisure trips rather than short distance commuting trips by automated vehicles.

In fact, advanced technologies have revolutionized many aspects of human life, include the automated vehicle transport system. Also, transport system is one of the essential development aspect to particular , such as non-manual driving automation , vehicle aims to make trips safer, faster , more efficient, automated vehicles passengers and drivers can feel enjoyable to do themselves leisure behavior , e.g. read books, listen, music, listen mobile, watch laptop movies when any one does not need to consider whether their cars are safe to be driven , even any one needs to drive the automated car, because robotic can help them to control how to automatic drive this car on the road safely.

Robotic will bring confidence to let them feel that themselves cars are moving safely on the roads . In recent years, the concept of automated driving has been introduced as on outstanding platform for the next generation of driving systems that is expected to improve safety, traffic flows efficiency, reducing traffic jams occurrence chance, avoiding traffic accidents occurrence chance, e.g. avoid to crash any one person when he/

she is walking across road or crach any car is moving on the road easily, capacity, accessibility , and reducing congestion through the application of some technologies , such as vehicle to vehicle and vehicle to infrastructure communication.

So, future automated vechicles can have good driving facility systems to be installed in their cars, in order to raise safety, rapid driving speed level to let any one to feel , when they are sitting in their automated cars, e.g. using cameras, sensors, global positioning system adaptive cruise control, light detection and ranging, and advanced driver assistance system, automated vehicles can steer the vehicle and drive it automatically when passengers delegate control to a computer. Absolutely, ny replacing the driver role with an automated driving system , future one automated vehicle is able to totally free up passengers under automation levels.

So, unless future any kinds of public transport tools may apply automated robotic automated driven system replace the bus driver, taxi driver, train driver, tram driver, underground train driver to raise automated driving system service improvement level to let any one passengers to feel. Otherwise, when automated vehicles are popular to be accepted to buy in any one country in global. Then, global public tansport tool passegners number may be influenced to reduce when global any one family owns at least one automated vehicle at themselves homes .

In other words, automated vehicles can bring thes benefits to let global any one household family feels, future automated vehicles users , they can mostly behave like passengers inside the vehicle, which implies that they will be able to multitask and productive by allocating the travel time to do other activities, e.g. reading, eating, working, drinking, watching movies, listening musics, even sleeping. So, automated vechicles will motivate humans to change non-humanly driven behaviors from conventional humanly driven behavior. This non-humanly driven behavior may be one main factor to influence or encourage future any one kind of public transport passenger won't choose to pay fare to buy ticket to catch any one kind of public transport tool again, because non-manual driven behavior may hel many lazy people do not need to consdierate how to learn to drive cars skills to prepare pass any road test in order to earn the driving licnece to permit to drive cars forever. When automated vehiclesa re popular to be accepted to replace manual-driven cars in societies.

Hence, automated vehicles could potentially change the traditional human driven vehicle market to cause their manual driven cars sale buyers number reduces, when the automated vehicle buyers number increases, also they can chance globa public transport passengers behaviors to reduce to pay fares to catch any kinds of public transport tools when automated vechicles users may sit on themselves automated vehicles to go to anywhere in short time rapidly and safely in any countries.

On conclusion, future global public transport service competition is serious, because instead of global passengers had began to compare whether which kinds of public transport fares are cheaper, more safe, shortening journey time between leaving place and destination, more comfortable feeling, e.g. clean and comfortable chairs , mre free internet service facilities in order to make any one kind of catching public transport tool choice in preference. On the other hand, future automated vehicles number will increase when traditional manual driven car users begin to believe that automated vehicles can bring more safe , more comfortable, more fee-time using, more leisure satisfactory feeling, more than traditional manual driving cars. Then, when global any one household family had made choice to buy at least one automated vehice to replace themselves car(s) at home. When, they are habit to sit in themselves automated vehicles to go to anywhere, however, short or long trip . Consequently, global any one household family won't feel any kinds of public transport tools may bring personal economic saving cost, comfortable, enjoyable, free-time using benefit to compare themselves automated vehicles . It will cause global public transport tools passengers number will reduce , when many different kinds of home automatic vehicles are purchased to replace manual driving cars by global household automated vehicle users. So, in passegner transport tool choice psychological view, automatic vehicles will be possible to replace future public transport service tools. So, any public transport service providers can not neglect how to desing and improve their facilities , charge reasonable transport fare, provide more comfortable, and enjoyable sitting feeling , even applying automatic driving system to replace human drivers in order to attract passegners ' catching need choice more easily.

Reference

Bailey, L., Mokhtarian, P.L. Little, A. (2008). The broader Connection Between Public Transportation, Energy Conservation And Greenhouse Gas Reduction, Report Prepared As Part Of TCRP Project J-11/Tasks Transit

Cooperative Research Program, Transportation Research Board Submitted To American Public Transportation Association in http://www.apta.com/research/into/online/land_use.cfmi, accessed 17 April 2008.

The UK Standing Advisory Committee On Trunk Road Assessment (SACTRA) (1999). Transport And The Economy (Report To UK DETR). Retrieved From: http://webarchive.nationalarchives.gov.uk/20050301192906 ; http://dft.gov.uk/stellent/groups/dft-econappr/documents/pdf/dft_econappr_pdf_022512.pdf

Wikipedia Contributors (2008). Arterial Roads In Wikipedia, The Free Encyclopeda, http://en.wikipedia.org/w/index.php?title=Arterial_road&oldid=212832640(accessed May30,2008).

How does (AI) robots' brain invention influence our lives?

(AI) research modeling the human brain has developed important technologies, and has overcome significant barriers. How will (AI) affect humanity in the near future? How will (AI) change our lives and our societies? Is the evolution of (AI) to humanity, or it represent a threat?

On white collar workers (AI) job replacement aspect, University of Tokyo, Institute of informatics, lecturers who had attempted to do experiments to take (AI) exams over a two year period. The (AI) achieved standard scores of around 50 in each subject, exceeding the norms for humans attempting the tests. The (AI)'s results in subjects emphasizing memorization, such as world history and Japanese history subjects were comparatively high, and the results of the study suggested that an appropriate selection of subjects would give at an 80% chance of passing the entrance exams of 80% of Japan's private universities.

So, if (AI) is applies to human white collar workers' job duties aspect, at this level, if white collar workers were replaced by (AI) in the future, around 30% of current staff would be replaced. Whatever, the outcome, large companies will be represented with two choices. One choice will be to protect their employees, but as a result lose their international competitiveness. The latter choice will enable them to reduce the cost of general duties, financial management procedures, accounting etc. general administrative job duties of cost in offices. Hence, it seems that (AI) will be possible to be invented to own human's brain ability to do some mind jobs in future on day.

However, the method called " deep learning" must be developed to cause (AI) to match human's brain ability as well as these were dramatic advances in technologies, such as image recognition and voice recognition, which form the foundation for (AI). Nowadays, this new method called" deep learning" does not reach the matured and stagnated stage. It needs to wait human to continue to invent to let (AI) to match human brain to achieve 100% owning human's mind ability. Nowadays, (AI) industry product include cleaning robots, smart TVs and future (AI) product development market. It will include self-driving vehicles, drones, and nursing robots.

On (AI) weapons applied aspect, if (AI) can be invented to own human's brain judgement and analytical abilities. Then, it is possible that it can be applied to attack enemy to cause war effect. For example, if weapons such as missiles were equipped with (AI) in the future, they would become able to decide on their own targets. Hence, human needs to apply restrictions when necessary.

On (AI) applied to analyzing information collected technological aspect, nowadays, every one will use wearable terminals to connect to the internet to obtain various types of information as well as computers will collect and analyze information on people. Our lives will probably be more reliant on these internet technologies than they are on smartphones today. When, (AI) can match human brain to own mind ability.

Then, (AI) can be applied to do any analyzing information and collection job duties aspect to raise large information restoring and remembering efficiency. For example, (AI) will be generally used and will be extremely useful in analyzing the information collected from wearable devices and stored in the cloud. (AI) will enable wearable devices to be of real assistance in our lives offering their users more intelligent support.

Rather than allowing (AI) to develop on serves, as something separate from humanity. It will be more meaningful to encourage its development via wearable devices, situating it under the control of human intelligence. The intelligence of (AI) will increase rapidly in the future. If this increase in (AI) occurs under human control, enabling humans to increase their own abilities, then surely it will be possible for us to put up a degree of resistance to the opposite scenario, the domination of (AI) over humanity. Hence, if (AI) can be invented to remember and store and make analytical judgement to collect any information from internet. Then, it will bring the effect, such as large international organizations' (AI) internet storage robots can bear in mind factors, such as competitors' privacy or business secret information, such as the loss equality between people and threats to privacy that will be stolen form the owning (AI) storing internet information remembering robots.

Consequently, what is the effect of successful invention of (AI) matching human brain's mind ability? (AI) present computers are adequately able to reproduce the emotional, conceptual and intuitive abilities of humans. Because of this, it is important that we should envision potential future problems that may manifest when we consider how to employ wearable devices. It will be essential to enhance our technologies in order to ensure that we can use (AI) under human control.

However, when a goal has been set. (AI) will implement an appropriate means for its realization. (AI) will be need as a tool by human society. If the capacities of analytical and judgement mind abilities of (AI) brain exceed those of human brain, it is difficult to imagine the type of technological, then singularity is represented by the creation of an (AI) by another (AI). It is important that we rapidly and accurately predict these developments, when image recognition and other individual technologies are functioning at a high level. There will be a considerable matter in different sectors of (AI) industry development.

Today, however, machines have become able to decide for themselves what they will learn, making it difficult to copy human's mind ability. What we must consider when machines exceed humans and (AI) surpasses human capabilities. May technologies exceed human capabilities, cars are faster than humans, planes are able to fly. Consequently, it brings a question that human needs to consider: When does (AI) brain technology be invented to reach the most reasonable stage to be accepted or stopped by humanity?

What is artificial intelligence
human brain invention?

A machine is likely to achieve the ability of a human brain. Does it a scientific story? Some scientists has predicted that a US$1,000 personal computer will match the computing speed and capacity of the human brain by around the year 2020 year. With human reverse engineering, human should have the software insights before 2030 year. it is possible that of machine intelligence and exotic new technology for faster and more powerful computational machines from cellular automata and DNA playing cheese game competition case example, it proves that (AI) had been invented to own human's analytical and judgement ability to exceed the best cheese game human player's brain analytical and judgement ability. Then, it seems that (AI) will have possible to be built machine brains to achieve the exceed level of human brain's analytical and judgement ability in the future one day.

Supposing we scan someone's brain and restate the resulting " mind file" into suitable computing medium. Will the entity that emerges from such an operation be conscious? How have advances in electronic communications changes power relationship? For electronic book publishing case example, a book that looks at the principles companies must adopt to meet the needs and desires of this new kind of client. So, such as paper book can be changed to electronic book for human to read. Why can't human brain be changed to (AI) machine brain to do human's analytical mind and behavioral mind of activities to replace to do any human's daily analytical and behavioral mind activities?

Over the next few decades, machine achieve super intelligence, human will encounter a dramatic phase. Will it be a "WALL" a barrier as conceptually the event of a black hole in space. Such as (AI) brain invention case, an " AI singularity" ruled super-intelligence AIs, or a gentler " surge" into a post human era of agelessness and super-intelligence brain. Will future technology, such as bio-engineered pathogens, self replicating nan robots, and super smart robots run and accelerate out of control, perhaps threatening the human race?

If one day, (AI) brain is invented to achieve agelessness possibility. It means human's brain will be old to lose mind and analytical ability when human's age is increasing. Otherwise, (AI) machine brain age won't lose mind and analytical ability, due to (AI) machine is no age increasing possibility. It is a machine brain. If (AI) machine brain can be built successfully. Scientists need to consider technological ethic matter, such as the challenge of guiding nanotechnology in a constructive direction, advances in nanotechnology and related advanced technologies can not be inevitable, any broad attempt to relinquish nanotechnology would interfere with the benefits. When actually making the dangers worse.

Keeping in mind that intelligence machines are already making their way into our blood stream. There are dozens of projects underway to create blood-stream based " biological micro electronic- system" (bio MES) with a wide range of diagnostic and therapeutic applications BioMEMS devices are being designed to intelligently pathogens and deliver medications in very precise ways. For example, a researcher at the University of Illinois at Chicago has created a ting capsule with pores measuring only seven nanometers. The pores let insulin out in a controlled manner, but prevent antibodies from invading the pancreatic Islet cells inside the capsule. These nano- engineered devices have cured rated with type I diabetes, and there is no reason that the same methodology would fail to work in humans. Similar systems could precisely deliver dopamine to the brain patients, provide blood-clotting factors for patients with hemophilia and deliver cancer drugs directly to tumor sites. A new design provides up to 20 substance-containing reservoirs that can release their cargo at programmed times and locations in the body.

Another brain health technological related invention case, such as Kensall Wise, a professor of electrical engineering at the University of Michigan, who has developed a tiny neural probe that can provide precise monitoring of the electrical activity of patients with neural disease. Future designs are expected to also deliver drugs to precise locations in the brain. Also, kazushi Ishiyama at Tohoku University in Japan has developed micro machines that use microscopic-cancer tumors.

A particularly innovative micro machine developed by Sandia National labs has actual micro teach with a jaw that opens and closes to trap individual cells and then implant them with substances, such as DNA, proteins or drugs. There are already at least four major scientific conferences on bio MES and other approaches to developing micro-and nano-scale machines to go into the body and bloodstream. All these inventions are related to how to apply machines to copy human's brain knowledge in order to achieve to do any human's brain functions.

Finally, for Freitas envisions micron-sized artificial platelets invention case example, who could achieve hemostasis (bleeding control) up to 1,000 times faster than biological platelets. Freitas describes nano-robotic microbivores (white blood cell replacement) that will download software to destroy specific infections hundreds of time faster than antibiotics, and that will be effective against all bacterial, and fungal infections with no limitations of drug resistance.

Consequently, such as above machine health scientific invention cases, there were many scientists had invented any health machines to apply drugs to transfer to human's brain to attempt to reduce human's disease causing risks, such as reducing cancer cell increasing number. Why it is no possible that scientists can attempt to invent (AI) brain which can own human's mind ability to judge or analyze any matters to give opinions in order to exceed human's judgement and analytical ability.

Printed by Libri Plureos GmbH in Hamburg,
Germany